The Preac'
V.

# A Woman's Perspective on Preaching

## Jane V Craske

ISBN  1 85852 181 5

*For Roy and Elizabeth Craske*

Jane Craske is a half-time tutor at Hartley Victoria College within the Partnership for Theological Education, Manchester, where she teaches courses in Christian theology, including 'Women and Theology'. She is also a minister in a half-time appointment in circuit in South Manchester. She co-edited *Methodism and the Future* (Cassell, 1999) with Clive Marsh.

# GENERAL INTRODUCTION

Preaching is a very particular form of communication which has always been important in the life of the Christian Church. At the beginning of the 21$^{st}$ century we are undergoing a revolution in the varieties, method and speed of our communications. Preachers of all denominations, ordained and lay, undertake this calling with an awareness that we preach in a changing context.

*The Preacher's Library* is designed to help us to think through, perhaps in some cases reassess, why we preach, how we preach, and to whom we preach. Some of the volumes in this series will take a fresh look at familiar issues, such as how preachers should approach various parts of the Bible, how we understand and express our doctrinal inheritance and the variety of styles in which preaching can be done. Other volumes will introduce issues which may be less familiar to many of us, such as the significance of our cultural context or the way in which the self-understanding of a woman preacher has important things to say to all preachers. Some of these books will offer direct help in the practice of preaching. Others will deal with issues which, although they appear more theoretical, impinge upon the preacher's task and on which we therefore need to have reflected if we are to preach with integrity in today's world.

All the writers in this series, lay and ordained, women and men, are recognised preachers within their own denominations and write with the needs of their colleagues firmly in mind. These books will avoid academic jargon, but they will not avoid dealing with difficult issues. They are offered to other preachers in the belief that as we deepen our thinking and hone our skills

God's people will be blessed and built up to the glory of God.

I have been asked, several times, why this series should include a book with the title *A Woman's Perspective on Preaching*. The reasoning behind the questions seems to be either that it could be of no interest to male preachers or, alternatively, that it does not make any difference whether a preacher is a male or female. The very asking of the question shows the need for the book! Jane Craske makes no claim to be writing a book about women's preaching, as if all women had the same experience or perspective. Indeed, she rightly rejects such stereotyping. What we are offered here is a sensitive, reflective and beautifully nuanced exploration of what it means to Jane that she is called to exercise a ministry of preaching, and that she does so as a woman. Why, then, should a man – or, for that matter, another woman – need to read it? Precisely because no preacher is a disembodied voice. What we are as human beings, including our gender and our sexuality, is an important part of who we are as preachers. When we recognise that we shall be better preachers, and Jane's perspective helps us to recognise it.

Michael J Townsend

# CONTENTS

# 1

# PERSONALLY SPEAKING

A woman's perspective

The title of this book is carefully chosen. In fact, the most pertinent word is probably the one readers may regard as least significant: 'a'. This book starts in a particular place, symbolised by the indefinite article, which is in this case quite definite in its identification of a singular space. I start from one perspective: mine. I hope that won't be where I end, but it has to be acknowledged as where I start.

Why is that so important? It is important for the sake of other words in the title. It sets up the personal perspective to counter any suggestion that it is possible to write about 'women's perspective' as if all women shared one way of experiencing the world, one way of looking at life, or as if all women preachers shared one way of preaching. The contrast is particularly important since it has been assumed for too long that women can be dealt with as a category rather than as individuals, and thereby looked at somehow from the outside.

*A Woman's Perspective on Preaching* is part of a series for all preachers. Though it starts from a personal perspective, consciously and deliberately, it is designed to reflect on the varied experiences of many. Because of the title, you may have begun reading expecting this book not to be about you, or not to have anything to say to you. That might be because you are a man, and you assume that anything with a title such as this must be not just about women, but for women. Or it might be because you are a woman who expects certain standard stereotypes about women from this book, which you do not expect to find congenial. But I am not writing a book for women only, either those who preach or those who don't preach.

This book does, however, explore a woman's perspective in the sense that my gender is a hugely important part of my identity, and, therefore, of my perspective on anything, including preaching. 'Who I am' is 'who I am as a woman'. As a Christian I am quite conscious of myself striving to be the person and the woman God has called me to be. Society makes me aware of my gender in ways that I will explore in more detail in chapter 2. It is as an embodied female that I preach and I have found over the years that attention has been drawn to that aspect of myself as a preacher in all sorts of ways. At a church in London which often saw visitors from a variety of countries and denominations, I often received comments which appreciated the presence of a woman preaching, as something still unusual, but welcome.

Part of what is going on both implicitly and explicitly as I write about myself, myself as a woman, other women's and men's experiences, and preaching, is that I am arguing that women must be seen as individuals, for whom gender is a crucial factor – as for men. Other factors will also be crucial parts of our identity: particularly ethnicity, class, sexuality and ability. I, however, have been asked to write with a gender perspective in mind and am not able to give space to the ways in which other categories of identity play their part. In particular, as a white woman, I cannot speak from the perspective of those for whom their identity as black women preachers is particularly important. That is why my perspective is not normative or prescriptive; it is not meant to be a pattern or a mould for anyone else. My perspective is simply illustrative. To start from my own standpoint is to develop a story which can be compared to that of others: to yours. Each of us is formed in many contexts, from our genes and our upbringing, our environment and our inheritance, but we take a unique, personal shape because above all we are God's creation made in God's image.

So this is a woman's perspective. The third word of the title is a further limiting factor and I have explored this language in more depth elsewhere.[1] To talk about perspectives is, for me, to talk in a metaphorical sense about particular, limited viewpoints. Words like 'viewpoint', 'standpoint' or 'outlook' share some of the same connotations, but 'perspective', for me, crucially adds an association about our involvement in reflecting on and even creating what we see and experience. I want to value those particular perspectives and the personal experiences that have shaped them, and also acknowledge their limitations. These perspectives are part of the truth that we search for and create, but they must be open to testing and critique.

I do not want to set up here an exaggerated individualism, according to which the individual's perspective cannot be challenged, or cannot be changed. Our perspectives are transformed by all sorts of things, often by being open to the perspectives of others. It has to be acknowledged that this is not always an egalitarian process. Some voices and experiences are given more weight than others. A voice in print is often given an exaggerated weight: the opportunity to reflect publicly on any subject is a position of privilege, because such public reflection may help form the perspectives of others. But this voice should be critiqued as any other.

However, I have used much personal language because I have also sought to be particularly careful with my choice of language when I expand my terms beyond my own perspective. Sometimes the language then gets woolly – 'some women', 'many women'. 'Some women' in each context means those who feel that their understanding and experiences can be expressed in these terms. But the phrasing is an attempt implicitly to acknowledge the experiences of those who don't see things in these terms. The dialogue going on in this book is not one between women and men, but between those women and men on the one hand who see Christian faith in a way that takes account of gender issues, and on the other hand those women and men who don't. So my personal perspective is based on experience, and on the belief that experience is to be valued in all reflection, but it is not intended to be necessarily a privileged perspective over against others.

Those who preach always preach in context – and that has at least two senses. It refers to what is going on around the preacher at the time of preaching – the church building, the congregation, the roadworks outside, the crèche at the back of church; as well as what is going on for the various members of the congregation. Here I am particularly concerned with another sense – that of the personal, social and faith contexts of the preacher herself or himself. We live within a multiplicity of contexts, intellectual, spiritual, geographical, relational. This book is an attempt to give voice to some aspects of those contexts, governed by the subject of gender relations. Each chapter highlights a different kind of context in which preaching happens. Most are entitled 'relating to . . .'. I use that style of title as a metaphor drawn from the most basic area of our lives: our relationships to other people. It implies the activity of relating, of working out where we stand in relation to people, or ideas or institutions, and how we are affected by them. Such relationships might be a matter of similarity or difference, contrast or correspondence, dependence, independence or interdependence. After all, working out how to move relationships forward forms a major part of our lives. I also want to indicate something of the juggling we do (and which, some assert, women do in particular), working on relationships with a variety of people or contexts or activities, all at the same time.

Each of us, with our own contexts, is distinctive. But that does not mean that we are wholly dissimilar from all others. We have things to share and compare. There are things we recognise in others' stories, as well as things we find strange. The popularity of biography as a category of literature has to do with our fascination with other people's stories, and our search for both similarities and dissimilarities with others. Above all, because we are human we are interdependent and connected one with another.

This writing is not, I have to say, backed up with carefully controlled primary research, involving either lots of people, or in-depth exploration with a few. However, I have tried to hear the experiences of a limited number of women who preach, through questionnaires and through conversations. That means there are no statistically valid conclusions to share here, but the questionnaires and conversations have revealed experiences that perhaps at the moment can only be described through story, anecdote, rumour, 'jokes' and misconceptions. These are often the only ways to begin to locate positive and negative stereotypes. This is the impressionistic realm of personal perceptions, but we have learned in recent years how much we have to gain by listening to those whose stories have not always come to the fore in the past.

## A personal context

The danger of exploring personal context is that of appearing self-indulgent and individualistic. I have already made much use of the word 'personal', but I distinguish that from the word 'individual'. For me, the latter term has associations with the person who believes they stand independent of everyone else. That is not to me an adequate account of personhood, because we become who we are through relationships. I am not meant to be writing autobiography either. However, it is an important theoretical starting point for me that we need to be as explicit about and as aware as possible of our own particular circumstances. In her book about theological education, Rebecca Chopp acknowledges, 'This book is written out of my own journey, as all books are crafted out of the writer's life.'[2]

I was born into and grew up within village Methodism, though the village was relatively large and in the London commuter belt, so it wouldn't be what you might perhaps associate with the words 'village Methodism'. Moreover my parents had experienced and valued various forms of Methodism in other parts of the country and told me stories of those. In that village church, those who were formative in my development as a Christian were Sunday School teachers, a youth group leader and local preachers. (I have relatively few memories of ministers as I was growing up.) At a fairly young age I was attending evening services because I enjoyed listening to sermons, and to particular preachers. The majority of preachers in that circuit, and all the ministers (up to 1999) were men. Our circuit was not unusual in that. I remember a few notable women preachers, particularly the two women we asked to preach at what I guess were Sunday School anniversary services one year. As members of the youth group we were asked to be involved in the planning of the evening service.

My family were and are steeped in Methodism: all my immediate family are still in the Methodist Church and have between them held most of the offices going. From the point of view of preaching, my father is a local preacher. I always thought him a very good preacher and spent most of my formative years quite sure that I could never preach like that. I recalled that in the sermon I preached, at his request, when he was presented with a certificate marking 40 years as a local preacher! It was at services led by my father that I first took part in worship by reading the Bible and singing.

I had an interest from an early age in history, and I have always enjoyed the sort of study which revealed more about the Christian tradition from a historical perspective. On the other hand, I am not a Church historian by specialism. Beyond that, I studied literature most keenly, alongside linguistics, and so have a particular love for words and books, and an appreciation of the power of words and the creativity with which they can be used. A further strand in my make-up is a view of the world through feminist perspectives and commitment. I explore that further in chapter 2, but it is worth noting here that I was learning about secular and Christian feminism at about the same time as I was beginning to preach.

It was at university that I was invited to join a preaching team, taking services on the local circuit plan under the nominal supervision of a minister and the actual supervision of a local preacher on trial who was a fellow student. It was in that situation, having found that 'I could do this' in the most minimal of senses, that I had to wrestle with the question of whether I was being called by God through that first experience of teamwork in the leading of worship, to the more traditional pattern (as I saw it) of 'solitary' local preaching.

Given a note to preach, my supervisor was a woman. However, I have to admit that I did all too little work with her since my experience with the university team was deemed sufficient for me to be out on my own almost immediately. I was a local preacher, on note, on trial and fully accredited for six years, preaching in at least four different circuits, before I entered training for ordained presbyteral ministry. I then preached in another five circuits, for a further six years before ordination. The different circuits covered cities, towns and villages, from East Anglia, to the Midlands, the North East and London. From quite early on in my preaching I became used to comments after I had led worship that centred on my age and my voice, and (before training for ordination) confirming congregation members' suspicions that I was a teacher. Make of that what you will – though I have heard preachers who are not teachers complain that everybody thinks they are. Only in one circuit did I regularly lead worship and preach with another colleague, at best after long discussions so that there was a genuine joint preparation involved.

I was conscious of being called as a preacher before any call to ordination, and that is probably significant in how I regard preaching. It was a shock to me in theological college to realise this was not the same for everyone! However, the pattern of my preaching is now determined in large part by the place I am in as an ordained minister, preaching regularly to one congregation who 'own' me as 'their' minister, and visiting another eight congregations on a more or less frequent basis.

In terms of the practice of preaching – particularly my style of preaching – I don't think I am a particularly radical preacher; and I am certainly not a satisfied preacher. I am heartened by Thomas Troeger writing: 'Effective preachers keep searching for their true voice.'[3] I find myself trying to experiment most of the time within a recognisable framework, and I'm conscious that I still rely heavily on words as the main vehicle for worship.

This particular woman's perspective comes out of such a background. Why is that important? Because I am concerned that all preachers should be aware of their own context, aware of the factors that have shaped them, their preferences and their prejudices. I am concerned that preachers should acknowledge the experiences and the needs which feed their theology and their practice of preaching.

## ... On preaching

I do not want to define preaching at this stage, since that might act as an inappropriate limitation on what I shall explore as the book progresses. Yet I need to signal some of the concerns or assumptions about preaching that are part of my perspective. I do it here by referring to the work of others and noting a few definitions or ideas that have helped me to think about my own preaching. I do it briefly, for I hope to build pictures of the preaching I want to aim for as I go along: pictures which arise in part out of reflection on women's experiences of the world, of the Church and of preaching. No work on preaching is new, and any writer acknowledges debts to other writing that has gone before. But it is still an interesting experience, from my perspective, reading the 'textbooks' on preaching that have been influential in their own time. Let me simply note here how recent appears to be the phenomenon of writing about preaching as if women as well as men might be preachers. Books written up to even the beginning of the 1980s continue to refer to preachers as male, some assuming that such language includes women, some quite clearly not envisaging women as preachers. (This also intersects in some books with the assumption that all preachers are ordained, which is another 'exclusive' assumption as far as Methodists are concerned.) Most recently a few self-consciously feminist works will probably outrage many by referring to preachers as 'she' throughout, but that does point up the usual fare. Part of my task in looking from a woman's perspective at preaching is to ask whether what has been said about preaching in general is indeed appropriate to women preachers as well as to men – whether it is truly or falsely universal.

In *Imagery for Preaching*, Patricia Wilson-Kastner describes her own framework for preaching: 'Preaching is that part of liturgical prayer in which the preacher, for the community, proclaims before God our remembrance of God's saving acts in the past, our awareness of divine presence here and now, and our response to God in our lives.'[4] Such a framework helps to situate preaching in the whole act of worship, so I hope that readers will bear this important context in mind if from now on I seem to deal with preaching in a strangely 'out of context' way in relation to worship. That is a necessary limitation of the task I have been given in writing this book. Wilson-Kastner's framework is helpful in illuminating a relationship of past/tradition, present/presence, and future/responsive action. I would want to add something that brings out more clearly the congregation's part in preaching (rather than the image of preaching simply happening 'before' the congregation), but the sense of preaching as proclamation, in a community, as part of the wholeness of the liturgy, is a good place to start.

Then, in Colin Morris' *Raising The Dead*,[5] there is a thread which I found myself tracing, to do with the preacher as individual, which I think relates to my own starting point in 'a perspective'. For Morris (advising a young preacher), the preached gospel is fashioned out of the preacher's distinctive and shared qualities (p.6). In my terms, there is light to be shed on the shared contexts out of which the uniqueness of personal context is shaped. 'And yet . . . here is a paradox. The preacher having asserted his or her individuality must then forget, even transcend it' (p.9-10). The business of preaching is about self-projection, but not exhibitionism (p.88). For me, 'transcending' individuality seems a more useful concept than 'forgetting'; or, better, allowing individuality to be transcended through the work of God and the congregation as a whole. Something particular, something valuably unique, is expressed in one person, through whom God may be perceived to be speaking, as the congregation responds both to what is unique to the preacher, and what is shared with them.

Susan White describes the overarching story of the late 20th century, the story which explains the way most people in Britain, at least, interpret their world, as 'the narrative of the free market economy'. There would seem to be little space for Christian preaching. Yet she argues, 'Christian preaching can be the most potent way of presenting an alternative to this free market world-view: a counter narrative around which new lives and a new social order can be established.'[6] That is an appropriately ambitious vision for preaching, with which I would like to be associated. It links us to the public world, and refuses to allow preaching to be insular, concerned only with the few who choose to be in church listening to sermons.

My final idea or direction in sketching what preaching might be about comes from Gerd Theissen's book, *The Sign Language of Faith*. He suggests, in a chapter on this subject, that the theological dimension of preaching is the way in which preaching offers people the opportunity to enter into dialogue with God. In fact that is not just the opportunity of preaching, it is the fundamental task of preaching. 'Any sermon lives on the hope of enabling contact to be made between God and human beings.'' Some of the dialogue will be, on our part, the offering of thanks and praise; some will be the offering of lament and anguish, some the offering of our questions . . . and much more.

These, then, are the different facets of my initial reflections on preaching. They are concerned with preaching in the Christian community, with the preacher, with the public world of which the Church is a necessary part, and with the search for God on which all else is founded.

Having described something of the particular perspective from which these reflections arise, in chapter 2 I take a detour from the usually all too church-based activity of preaching and explore how preachers relate to the society around them, in particular to the gender stereotypes and conflicts in various societies, here illustrated by the context I know best: modern Western culture in Britain. I return to more obvious themes with a focus on the Bible in chapter 3, reflecting in particular on some women's difficulties either with particular texts or with the Bible as a whole. Chapter 4 tackles the realm of personal spirituality under the heading 'relating to Jesus'. In chapter 5 I have tried to explore a whole range of things that arise particularly from the stories I have heard about how women preachers are received in the churches at the turn of the 21$^{st}$ century. Then with chapter 6, I try to describe my vision for preaching in the light of engagement with these various contexts. In a brief epilogue I tackle whether women's preaching is anything different from men's preaching. Through it all I hope to engage the reader in rewriting/reflecting on these issues from his or her own perspective.

# 2

# RELATING TO SOCIETY

## S ocial context

The responsible preacher, I suggest, is one who knows the importance of being aware of her or his contexts. One of those contexts is the cultural and socio-political scene that surrounds us. The Church may not be 'of the world', but it is certainly 'in the world', and, however much we might want to add other dimensions to any definition, the Church takes its place *at least* as a social and cultural institution. This context must, of course, be further specified. I can only write with regard to modern British society, aware that even that particular society will look very different to different people. Again, my reflections are intended as a stimulus to those of the reader. I make the assumption that the kind of reflection on that society which I suggest below will be undertaken with Christian presuppositions.

Preachers proclaiming the deeds and promises of God before the Christian community must, to state the obvious, keep their eyes on the world around in order to relate the proclamation and its consequences to the everyday lives of Christians relating to the society in which they live. We may have been told, as preachers, to prepare worship with the Bible in one hand and the newspaper in the other. That will involve us in thought and debate about politics in all its aspects, from global concerns to local, about education, about how neighbours live together in the richness of multi-cultural experience, or in the face of

12

crime. We need to consider scientific advancements as intelligently as possible, and the dilemmas of the medical or the business world, and to what extent the family patterns of various societies are really changing, for better or worse. We are not expected to be experts in all these fields, but we are expected to be interested, and not so fixed in our opinions that we cannot learn more. To be fascinated by God is to be fascinated by the world.

Any attention to the newspapers, and so to current debates in society, will bring us up against the relationships between men and women. On the day after the A-level results were published in 1999 (20th August), the *Sun*'s headline was: 'It's *A* girls' world: They beat boys in best-ever exams'. The *Daily Mail*, on the other hand, interpreted the results differently: 'Boys are back on top of A-level league'. Notice the results are not 'simply' being reported but have become part of a debate about the relative achievements of boys and girls in the British educational system. It's also clear from the two different examples of headlines that the way this debate is perceived is more a matter of interpretation than of indisputable facts. Reporting of the results in 2000 followed a remarkably similar pattern.

A headline in the *Guardian* proclaims: 'Labour scorned for failing to select women' (16th October, 2000) over a front page article, followed by two further pieces and a leader comment on local Labour parties' apparent unwillingness to select women as prospective parliamentary candidates. (A careful reader might want to ask why that headline when the article also discusses the same phenomenon with ethnic minority candidates, and in fact highlights the cases of two black women.) In the same day's paper was an article on women who are farmers and their usual invisibility.

All of these issues are really part of a much wider debate, which has been part of human life for hundreds of years in some form or other, about the relative abilities of women and men, and about the roles appropriate for them to play in society. It is not hard in almost any daily newspaper to find stories that are being read through the issue of whether or how men and women differ from one another, and what the consequences of difference might be. Often what determines a story about a particular person – present or past – is the extent to which that person is seen to be defying stereotypes.

Therefore, the Church, and particularly its preachers, must be attentive to gender relations as one important issue that we face in our social context, though not to the exclusion of all others.

**Stereotypes**

A circuit-wide 'younger women's meeting' which I attended listened to a black woman analysing her perceptions of an incident that had taken place in church some while before. She, and others in the congregation, had felt greatly offended at what they felt was the use of racist stereotyping. As the conversation among the women flourished towards the end of the meeting, it became clear that it was not just racist stereotypes that were of concern, but also sexist stereotypes – in the church, you will notice. Again and again stereotypes about women are heard, in sermons in particular, usually as illustrations. There are stories that assume women to be looking after children in the home; there are stories about over-anxious, nagging wives, about women who (of course) can't resist shopping. Many of these are supposed to be jokes, I will be told. I report, in contrast, my own anger and the anger of others at the use of these old-fashioned, stereotyped ideas which seem to trap some women by binding them round with prescribed, limited expectations.

The other side of stereotyping is the apparent invisibility of women, or women's experiences, in some church discourses. Even classic textbooks on preaching prove their age, and their closeness to their culture (even more stereotyped 50 years ago), at this point. W E Sangster, in his book on sermon construction, reels off a list of possible analogies . . . 'Life as a voyage; Life as a cricket match; The devil as a bowler; The Christian life as a military campaign; The Church as an organism . . .'[1] The majority of those are images which he would have imagined have a much closer connection to men's experience than to women's, and women remain invisible. I'm not sure that these images would have been balanced by others more relevant to other sections of the congregation, either by one preacher, or by other preachers. An even more revealing example comes in his discussion of the preacher's reading of fiction: 'They may not be "best-sellers". The book which "everybody is talking about" his wife will probably read, and she can tell him "the tale". It is amazing what time an intelligent woman can save a busy man in this way'.[2] More than the face value of the remark, what is obvious also behind it is the assumption that the preacher is male, and that his wife's intelligence is perfectly properly spent in reading 'best-sellers', while his is not. Using 50-year-old examples, however, may begin to show the dramatic ways in which susceptibilities have changed.

The English word 'stereotype' has its origin in the printing industry, as a printing plate cast from a mould taken from moveable type. Therefore the figurative (and now more usual) meaning is that 'to stereotype' is to fix something that was once moveable and establish it in an unchanging and unchangeable form. Stereotypes abound in our language and other cultural forms. They are a kind of shorthand, a cartoon, admitted to be slightly inaccurate – at best. At worst they can be imprisoning, because people have used them so often that they have come to believe them, and expect the stereotyped object to behave in the stereotyped manner. Thus mothers-in-law must all be harridans (note: in the perceptions of their sons-in-law), and all football fans are male (one I take particular exception to)! More seriously, research discussed in *New Scientist* (30th September, 2000) goes beyond arguing that negative stereotypes can be hurtful. Various pieces of research suggest that stereotypes affect how we think about ourselves, to the extent of affecting behaviour, so that exposure to negative stereotypes is shown negatively to affect how people behave in intelligence and other tests.[3]

Any group asked to 'brainstorm' masculine and feminine characteristics would quickly develop a lengthy list. Under 'masculine' they might have words like 'strong', 'active', 'competitive', 'aggressive', 'rational', 'logical', 'analytical'; under 'feminine' they might have words like 'gentle', 'peaceful', 'compassionate', 'unselfish', 'concerned with relationships', 'loving', 'intuitive', 'emotional' . . . But what relation do these words, which express certain stereotypes, bear to real life, or to real people? I remember doing an exercise in a racism awareness workshop where we were required to list all the stereotyping and insulting words we knew about black people. It was a painful exercise, but the point of it was to show us the kind of cultural associations that are part of the world we live in, the things that are in the back of our minds, somewhere. Similarly, we live in our social context with the knowledge of stereotyped patterns to which women and men have been expected to conform, at least in the past: assumptions about behaviour, about appropriate roles, which establish symbols of what it is to be a woman or a man. These patterns still govern many of the ways in which people are judged in today's world.

Some stereotypes about how women ought to behave are revealed in the horror expressed when such expectations are dashed. Why is our society so fascinated by women like Rosemary West and Myra Hindley? There are many more male serial killers in British prisons than there are female. But, I suggest, we focus less on them because somehow women who kill are thought to transgress their 'natural' behaviour patterns far more severely than men. Statistically men are more likely than women to kill. The attention focuses on those individuals who fail to fall in with the stereotype of women's behaviour as gentle, peaceful, more likely to be victim than aggressor. I am not supporting or excusing any particular moral view of transgressive behaviour, but simply pointing out the gender implications and the stereotyping in the way we react.

Joan Smith notes '. . . the received wisdom which holds that women are very different from men but the same as each other'.[4] This is a step further than basic ideas about stereotypes. It is what I referred to in chapter 1 as the treating of women as all in one category, such that, for instance, the one woman preacher felt by some to be less than acceptable is regarded as reflecting on all women who preach. With a few moments' thought we recognise such an assumption as unintelligent, of course, but we are in the area of half-conscious reactions here. Women preachers can't be heard as well; they don't preach incisively; they're not tall enough for our pulpits; they have to be careful how they dress . . . Whatever the comment is, it is being used of 'women preachers' in general (whether the comment is one that men or women use, or whether it is taken to be a negative or positive comment) in a way that would not be done quite as easily with men.

Stereotypes about women and about ministry were challenged in a light-hearted way through the TV series *The Vicar of Dibley*. Perhaps it doesn't have much to say to preaching, since Geraldine was only rarely seen in the pulpit, with a choice few sentences from a sermon deemed enough for dramatic purposes! Whether the series has itself created stereotypes (television being that powerful a medium) remains to be seen.

Many societies have begun to tackle the dangers of stereotypes, and the offences they cause to people who feel their lives are damaged by them. Some dismiss that process and damn it with the label 'political correctness'. Others are finding a freedom in being able to protest on the grounds of wanting to be able to define themselves instead of having to live with the unintelligent shorthand labelling of others.

## A framework for interpretation

It is not only in recent years that there have been complaints about stereotypes. Mary Wollstonecraft[5] wrote in the 18$^{th}$ century arguing against the presumption that in women the rational nature was subordinate to the 'sensible' (sensual and emotional). Her voice and those of a few others argued that the way women had been viewed was being used to discriminate against women, and keep them in an inferior place in society relative to men. The voices increased with campaigning for 'votes for women'. But even that was not enough and the voices became a flood with the 'women's liberation' movement of the 60s. Feminists argued, and still argue, that what has been deemed 'natural' for women (the stereotyping of what women should be and do) has often been simply a way of keeping them under the control of men, particularly in earlier ages keeping women's sexuality under the control of men.

Taking a historical perspective, it would be hard for anyone to argue that women have never been discriminated against. Women have been treated as the property of men, and in many parts of the world still are, with few rights of their own to determine their lives. Is this of any relevance to the Christian Church? Certainly, since it has often been Christian teaching – that women have a particular, limited place in society, that this is 'natural', determined by God at creation, or at least after the Fall – which, in Christian cultures, has kept women in places where they have been at risk of being undervalued, discriminated against and abused.

'Feminism' is the umbrella term for a range of theories which offer a framework of interpretation about human society, describing and analysing women's positions in various societies and seeking to transform them. Feminists have analysed discrimination chiefly under the word 'patriarchy', signifying the dualistic systems of the world which lie beneath discriminatory treatment, based initially on the perceived differences between women and men. It refers to systems of rulership, ways in which power is distributed in the world, which keep women within any society in the inferior position, even though the conditions of women's lives vary greatly from one society to another. Feminists have examined the different roles women and men have played in human society, arguing that those differences have been differently *valued*. Work from all sorts of academic disciplines might demonstrate this: 'Men may cook or weave or dress dolls or hunt humming birds but if such activities are appropriate occupations of men, then the whole society, men and women alike, notes them as important. When the same activities are performed by women they are less important.'[6] A lack of value for women's roles is yet associated with strong cultural pressures on both women and men to conform to expected roles within society, which chiefly hold women rather than men more closely to their biology. Women are to concentrate on their role in reproduction, looking after children and the home.

But relationships between women and men are not the only ones to which feminists pay attention: particularly in recent years, interlocking systems of oppression have been identified which deprive many people of power and opportunities in society. Discrimination may be based on categories of ethnicity, class or gender, sexuality or ability, and categories such as these will intersect in various ways for different people.

In 20th century Western societies, many of the traditional expectations of women began to break down, due in part to feminist analysis of their more destructive elements. At the beginning of the 21st century, that still leaves many people in uncertain situations, where relationships, roles, expectations and opportunities cannot be taken for granted, but must be thought about and sometimes renegotiated. That is not necessarily a comfortable position for all sorts of reasons. Some allege now a backlash against feminism, in a reassertion of traditional roles, or in more directly antagonistic behaviour against women, especially women in the workplace. Others note that women have still not achieved equality in many spheres of life, while still others deny that equality is a realistic or preferable aim.

'Feminist analysis over the last two decades has highlighted the extent of the inequalities women suffer, and it calls for some kind of reaction. The committed feminist will be angry, the committed anti-feminist will either deny that women are disadvantaged, or believe it serves them right.[7] Feminism is still a word which evokes much disquiet, in my experience particularly in the Church. Christians could have any of the reactions suggested in the quotation above, or additionally the idea that differentiated roles for men and women are part of God's plan, so the notion that either women or men are advantaged or disadvantaged by that must be a myth. If we are prepared to recognise it, then the debate about gender relations and the way we should interpret certain phenomena in our society *is already there in the church*, simply because members of church congregations are part of society. Yet it seems the debate only comes to the fore when people can no longer avoid it, as in discussions over the use of so-called 'sexist' language in church. Even then, many people are unwilling to delve into the underlying issues.

I hear the statement made not infrequently, if gender issues are raised in churches, that there isn't any discrimination any more, and there certainly isn't any (and hasn't been for years) in the Church. Very often it is women who make such assertions. Many women will argue (as a few black people do also with the issue of racism) that there cannot be any discrimination since they have experienced none. Even though I defend a theology rooted firmly in experience, I believe also in the testing of our own theologies and theories against the experience of others, including those who do believe they have suffered discrimination.

Feminism has been particularly feared within Churches when it is seen as posing a threat to family life. The assumption behind that fear is that stable family life depends on certain gender patterns. Certainly in its earliest 1960s' manifestations feminism was more inclined to encourage women to take up roles different from that of wife and mother, often devaluing the role of women who 'chose to stay at home', seeing that as an inherently imprisoning and destructive role for women. Various forms of feminism did change, however! By the end of the

1970s and into the 1980s there were several shifts. One was the greater emphasis on choice for women – such that exercising choice was valued more than what the choice actually was. But also, women's differences from men themselves came to be valued more greatly. Rather than attempting some kind of blurring of the distinctions between women and men, many feminists argued for a re-valuation of the different roles. (From this came the stereotype that feminists saw women as better than men – and simply sought to reverse discrimination.)

Does this really touch our lives? I have led a privileged life in all sorts of ways, and if I wanted to point to severe discrimination, I would look at the lives of other women. But I am also daily involved in gender issues when I fear men walking past me on the street in the dark, and alter my life according to that fear; when I feel degraded and frightened by being whistled at or having comments shouted at me in the street; when my life choices and Christian discipleship are questioned because I have chosen to be childless, though I am married; when I am still frequently addressed under male terms in the Church; when I try to work out what is or isn't discrimination in the male-dominated profession/ vocation I belong to, which (more than 25 years after the ordination of women in the modern British Methodist Church) still appears to be worldly enough to have a distinct glass ceiling for women.

Feminist theories provide one sort of framework for understanding gender relations in society, though they are not the only possible framework. Feminism is given prominent place here because among all its various theories are many that I have found convincing. So often in society at large I find the assumption that any argument there was about women's equality has been won, and there is nothing more that needs transformation. So often in the Church, I find the arguments have not even been aired, and there is much more the impression of wishing it would all go away. I do not believe that is the best we can do to engage, as Christians, with complex social issues.

## Where does this leave preaching?

What relevance does any of this have for preaching? I repeat my starting point, suggesting that any self-respecting preacher will want to be aware of these issues because that is one crucial part of relating to society. Many preachers will have lived through considerable social change in relations between women and men. The expectations of gender roles which someone now in their 70s grew up with are probably very different indeed from my own, as a preacher in her 30s, growing up and becoming conscious of feminism in the 1970s and 1980s. Some will recognise the great difference that the Second World War made to many women's expectations about employment, for instance. Some will have found the 1960s profoundly disturbing; others will have found them liberating. These are facets of our social context, to be reflected on in the light of Christian faith. They are also facets of our identity. They call for a response not just of detached interest, but of self-awareness and involvement.

Within their personal contexts, preachers will decide how to respond to gender issues (though I continue to call with hope for dynamic engagement which at least recognises that the debate matters). Some will find feminist categories convincing; some will find them utterly unconvincing. But we are alike in needing space to choose and to label our own identity, with awareness of our social context, so that we understand more clearly what factors in our own history and in the society around us (including within the Church) have played their part in our formation. For all these factors will affect our preaching, and the more conscious we are of that, the more responsible we will be in our work.

Some women have complained that many of the issues that are important in their experience of the world are not reflected in worship, and especially not given voice in preaching. Have women's experiences of violence and abuse in the home been left unheard? Or the question of whether some biblical teaching is heard differently by men and by women; or the dilemmas of choices to be made about patterns of family life? Perhaps women who preach could develop links between Church and the caring professions, or the experience of juggling several activities at once, or oppression? It has been said that with a greater number of women preachers there is now a greater likelihood that the situation will change. Such suggestions are put forward particularly in situations where a greater number of women preachers are now emerging in the wake of decisions to ordain women. Here is a call for specific research: it would no doubt be interesting within a denomination where women have been preaching for a great number of years (though always in the minority) to test out any differences in voicing gender-specific experiences in preaching.

Yet the danger is that we have walked straight back into the dangerous language of stereotypes, or at least, back into the ambiguous land where women seem to have a lot in common, perhaps as the result of becoming used to (socialised into) the roles expected of them. If we reflect that in preaching or any other discourse, are we reinforcing stereotypes, or are we properly exploring women's present experiences? Similarly, is it a stereotype to imagine that these areas are the preserve of women preachers? But this is the complex territory in which we have to live. Generalisations that seem to be useful shorthand are often also grossly inaccurate. What we surely should seek instead is the creation of space where as many specific voices as possible are heard.

I am not naive enough to imagine that the call to reflect on social context, or on gender relations, in the light of Christian faith, will lead all preachers to the same conclusions. However, it seems to me there is one clear-cut call to preachers that comes out of this material about social context. I believe that the Christian gospel undermines all human hierarchies of domination. Whether or not we agree about precisely where discrimination and domination are being experienced in current British society, we can see the effects of oppression based on discriminatory attitudes and practices in our world as a whole. Christian preaching could and should be a continual challenge to oppressive societies, always attentive to the abuse and dehumanising of any for whom Christ died.

# 3

# RELATING TO
# THE BIBLE

'The Bible says . . .'

It should be clear by now that I am suspicious of many generalisations about women, even about their differences from men. But there is a factor here which it is important to face at the very beginning of this chapter, for it illustrates the fundamentally different place of women from men with regard to the Bible and preaching. The Bible says:

> Let a woman learn in silence with full submission. I permit no woman to teach or to have authority over a man; she is to keep silent. For Adam was formed first, then Eve; and Adam was not deceived, but the woman was deceived and became a transgressor.
>
> (1 Timothy 2:11-14)

> As in all the churches of the saints, women should be silent in the churches. For they are not permitted to speak, but should be subordinate, as the law also says. If there is anything they desire to know, let them ask their husbands at home. For it is shameful for a woman to speak in church.
>
> (1 Corinthians 14:33b-35)

The Bible contains texts forbidding women to speak in the churches; it does not have comparable texts about men. These verses have been enough to ensure that women preachers have been the peculiarity and the exception to the rule until very recently in the Christian Church, for they have been the biblical basis for refusing women permission to preach, until and including the present. All women preachers at some stage must face these verses.

For some women this is relatively easy: perhaps the current acceptance in most churches that it *is* within God's purposes for women to preach is enough to govern their interpretation of biblical verses such as those above. For others, these verses are interpreted as understandable within the culture in which they were written, but not to be applied directly to our very different culture. For other women who feel called to preach, wrestling with these verses will be a major part of understanding their calling.

Soon after I had received a note to preach, I met up with two school friends with whom I had been part of the school Christian Union. I told them of my testing of this call to preach, with some excitement. But one of them put me firmly in my place, by telling me I was mistaken, since God didn't call women to preach. Witness the relevant verses in the Bible. This was partly a disagreement about the Bible and its interpretation, but also a deep questioning of my religious experience. The two were inseparable, and although I thought I had come to some intellectual accommodation with the biblical passages concerned, I discovered I could still be easily undermined emotionally. The tie-up of the intellectual and the emotional are crucial here. Somehow my sense of self, and certainly my sense of myself before God was being attacked, using the words of the Bible.

I doubt if I am the only woman preacher (or the only Methodist woman preacher) to have had some similar experience, especially among those who claim to take a particularly 'high' view of biblical authority, who use the phrase biblical 'inerrancy', or who talk of a strict biblical literalism. This is a distinctive experience of women, because of their gender.

## Is the Bible for men?

At the end of the 19th century, as the culmination of a lifetime's reflection, study and protest, Elizabeth Cady Stanton published *The Woman's Bible*.[1] This was really a commentary on the Bible, edited by Stanton and written by a number of women scholars, although the largest amount was written by Stanton herself. Stanton believed that religious prohibitions were at the root of women's subordination in her society. She had experienced discrimination in various guises in her life, not least in the way in which women's work for the abolition of slavery was disregarded in the public arena. She could cite various prevailing arguments about women's status, nature and role – arguments about the wife having no rights over her husband in law; arguments against the use of anaesthetics in childbirth and the refusal of some churches to allow a woman to enter a church building without a head-covering – in all of which biblical passages were cited to underpin what she saw as the oppression of women. She challenged interpretations of the Bible over these issues on the ground that Christian communities had recently been able to countenance change in biblical interpretation: biblical texts which had previously been understood to support the institution of slavery were re-interpreted through new commitments to the abolition of slavery.

*The Woman's Bible* was not an attempt to provide a commentary on the whole of the Bible, but simply on those parts which had to do with women in particular, whether episodes in which women appeared, or laws or other pronouncements about women. 'Whatever the Bible may do in Hebrew or Greek, in plain English it does not exalt and dignify woman,'[2] she argued in her introduction. *The Woman's Bible* is easy to criticise: Stanton proves herself by today's standards (which are not themselves perfect) racist, classist and prudish, as well as all too apt to assume that her middle-class interpretation of what women are and want will suffice for all women. However, she raised questions about the Bible which were not tackled so explicitly again until the 1960s. Her writing is forthright, opinionated, dismissive on occasions, and shirks nothing.   Of the differences between the two accounts of creation in Genesis 1-2 she writes, 'It is evident that some wily writer, seeing the perfect equality of man and woman in the first chapter, felt it important for the dignity and dominion of man to effect woman's subordination in some way.'[3]  On the other hand, she uses her commentary on the Bible as commentary on her own society.  In writing about the story of the wise and foolish wedding attendants, she comments on women's devotion to the service of the Church: 'It is not commendable for women to get up fairs and donation parties for churches in which the gifted of their sex may neither pray, preach, share in the offices and honours, nor have a voice in the business affairs, creeds and discipline, and from whose altars come forth biblical interpretations in favour of woman's subjection.'[4]

Cady Stanton was nothing if not a radical in theology.  Because of the attitudes to women she saw displayed in the Bible, she argued that the Bible was clearly not divinely inspired, but had to be critiqued as simply the work of men.    For those of us who do retain an understanding of divine inspiration of the Bible, her work can still help us to ask questions about how the Bible prescribes the pattern of women's lives, shaping the way in which Christian women understand themselves.  The Bible may have far less influence in society at large than when Stanton was writing, but it certainly still underpins the opinions of many in churches about women's vocations.

**The Bible and the reader**

All preachers – men and women alike – begin as readers and interpreters of the Bible, in common with all Christian disciples. Relating to the Bible, therefore, begins before we come to look at the Bible as preachers and the primary question here for all of us is 'How do *I* read the Bible?'  I want to address first what we find in the Bible, and what we make of that collection of texts, as readers.

The places in which we stand, the social and personal circumstances in which we find ourselves, all play their part in our reactions to and understanding of the biblical texts. (That is a somewhat simplified definition of 'hermeneutics', which is the study of interpretation.) As a woman and as a feminist, I find myself particularly aware of how women are situated in the Bible. It has become part of my awareness of myself, and of myself as a woman, to look at the texts that make up the Bible through the spectacles of a sensitivity to gender issues. It is part of finding myself, created and saved by God, in the Bible – or not.

For me, however, that doesn't mean the kind of project that Cady Stanton took on, in which she paid attention only to those texts that mentioned women explicitly. I read all of the Bible, as a woman and as a human being. In critical and imaginative engagement with the Bible, gender is one perspective but it is not the only issue that informs my reading of the Bible. Sometimes attention to gender seems utterly irrelevant in my reading of parts of the Bible, but not (as some would suggest!) all the time. I would call this a committed reading of the Bible, and I believe all of us read the Bible in committed ways. However, this does not mean that we cannot see beyond our own commitments to new interpretations. All of us can learn from others who read the Bible through different eyes, who have particular perspectives on race or class, on sexuality or varying abilities.[5]

There are probably three aspects to the committed reading/interpreting of the Bible as it relates to gender issues. One is the highlighting of stories about women which are in the Bible but which may have been ignored or forgotten. This may include critique of precisely how particular passages have been interpreted. So, for instance, stories of Miriam, or Hannah or Deborah are remembered. Likewise the name of Joanna as a disciple of Jesus is recognised, while (my particular bugbear) the Church's traditions are taken to task over how *and why* we ever got a picture of Mary Magdalene as a reformed prostitute, since she appears by name only in Luke 8:2 (as a woman healed by Jesus) and in the passion narratives (faithfully staying by the cross and meeting the risen Christ).

A second activity in this particular committed reading is the highlighting of the abuse, the degrading and the absence of women in the Bible.[6] This is most obvious in stories which specifically portray the rape and murder of women (e.g. Judges 19; 2 Samuel 13). We ought to ask questions as readers about what purpose such stories serve, and what attitudes towards the stories is implicit in the narrative. Perhaps more controversial is the questioning of laws which enshrine the position of women as the property of men, or regulations which legislate for the control of women's sexuality. These too may be read as abusive of women.

I would also include in this aspect of Bible reading what some may feel merits a separate aspect altogether, which is the absence of women in so much of the Bible, or at best their being sidelined. The assembly of Israel in the Old Testament is constructed as male, which can be spotted through the occasional instances when women are mentioned specifically. Psalm 128 is the classic example of the expectation that those favoured by God are men. And theological arguments have been built on the absence of women in the Twelve – the core of Jesus' disciples. This absence, this denial of women's presence is part of the way in which the biblical tradition seems to devalue women. I am one of those prepared to name such devaluing as abusive. These are some of the things which make the Bible difficult. There are points at which, from our cultural position, blinkered though it may also be, we need to critique the biblical text. They are occasions for anger and for sadness.

To take one example: the children of Jacob/Israel to whom the Bible pays attention are his 12 sons. They are the 'founding fathers' of the 12 tribes of Israel. It is they who figure in the conflict and later reconciliation with Joseph which results in the family of Jacob going down to

Egypt. But Jacob also had a daughter, by his wife Leah. Her story is told in Genesis 34. Or perhaps it would be better to say that her story is not told. She is the victim of rape, an object of love, the object used to deceive the people of the region. She is not a character. In fact the story is about the relationships between the men of Jacob's family, and the men among whom they live. The daughter of Jacob has no choice, and no words. She is mentioned, abused, forgotten. It is not after all her story: it is a story of men. That is precisely the difficulty for some readers of the Bible. It appears to be the words and the stories of men, with women only the exceptions or 'the other' (those who are described from outside, from another perspective). For some people, that is enough for them to dismiss the Bible. Those of us who do not dismiss the Bible might take one of two options with such passages: the first is to ignore what is unsavoury; the second is to question the values of the biblical writers and thus, in one sense, subvert the Bible.

There is, in addition, a third strand for the committed reader who chooses to look at the situation in which women are placed by the Bible. Luise Schottroff writes: 'The most important school of justice I know is the biblical tradition',[7] which is her way of describing a strong strand of biblical material which undermines the oppressive power structures of the world. There is a choice of interpretation involved in highlighting this material, since there is undeniably much in the biblical corpus which simply maintains the status quo. But I, for one, need to find some way of acknowledging the life-giving, justice-making, revelatory, God-bearing side of the Bible, which is precisely what keeps those of us who also see an oppressive side to the Bible hanging on to it for dear life. So there is a side to the reading of the Bible through a gender perspective which recognises that women can be liberated by it.

This view of the Bible has been made easier for many by the historical work of Elisabeth Schüssler Fiorenza in *In Memory of Her*. Her thesis is that women disciples had a much more visible role in the Jesus movement, and women leaders a higher profile in the early Church than had previously been acknowledged by scholars. Fiorenza starts by being suspicious of biblical texts, expecting them not to be unbiased historical records, especially where women are concerned. Again, as with Stanton, this can be difficult for some Christian readers of the Bible. But, from that perspective, she points up differences of emphasis between Paul's letters and Luke's writings:

> The Pauline letters indicate that women have been apostles, missionaries, patrons, co-workers, prophets, and leaders of communities. Luke, on the other hand, mentions women prophets and the conversion of rich women but does not tell us of any instance of a woman missionary or leader of a church.[8]

Similarly, Luke's writings don't suggest that there was any conflict over women's roles in the early Church communities, but the epistles suggest that there was. For Fiorenza, this is part of her charting the gradual suppression of women's leadership through biblical texts. She also asks what significance there is to the very different accounts of resurrection stories, broadly similar in the gospels, in complete contrast to the (pre-Pauline) account in 1 Corinthians 15. Or, again, what is the significance in Christian history of Jesus never demanding women's submission to men (or to their husbands), in contrast to the household codes of later texts, reflecting the values of more settled Christian communities? Fiorenza's careful reading of biblical and other historical texts highlights dialogues, progression, disagreements within the Bible as texts, stories, passages are laid alongside each other.

Highlighting forgotten stories, critiquing abuse and rediscovering the liberating power of the gospel as witnessed in some biblical texts: all these are unashamedly aspects of committed reading, that is reading with awareness of the particular place any of us starts from, and reading with a sense of purpose. Readers who have been fascinated by the Bible will continually be exploring its richnesses, developing awareness of their own starting points, and moving beyond them to see how others read the Bible and what insights can be learned from other perspectives.

## The Bible and the preacher

The preacher starts off as a reader of the Bible. But then she or he is concerned not just to read and understand but to proclaim the message of God as it can be found through the testimony of the scriptures. This is a particular use of the Bible. How we preach will develop from our interpretative decisions, from what we think the Bible is about. Material such as my reflections above on one way of looking at certain parts of the Bible will inform what the Bible is about for us. But I do not mean to imply that we decide that in isolation as individuals. We read and preach within churches, within Bible study groups, through Faith & Worship training, and all these are Christian communities in which interpretation takes place. What we understand about the Bible will be decisively informed by what we have heard interpreted and preached by others, what we have been taught, the biblical studies that have made sense to us, within our theological context.

The Bible Society has now been promoting for a couple of years a programme called 'The Open Book'. It is an attempt to spur all Christians into opening the book of the Bible up to the culture in which we live and opening our culture to the Bible. This whole enterprise must, of course, be of particular concern to preachers. The programme focuses on major themes, all narrative strands of the one story of God's relationship with human beings and the earth. The strands this project highlights are: Creation (and therefore our common identity as men and women before God), Exodus (the theme of liberation), Exile and Restoration (highlighting the road to a just society), the Birth of Jesus Christ (hope and fulfilment for all), and the Death and Resurrection of Jesus (forgiveness and a new future). This scheme offers the challenge to us to develop enough knowledge of the Bible to build a picture of its major 'sweep' – the story of God creating, choosing, calling, interacting with people. The Bible also tells the story of human beings responding to God and failing to respond, while God continues to reach out, decisively for Christians in the incarnation, in the life, death and resurrection of Jesus.

This is the story that preachers tell, the gospel they proclaim week by week in (and outside) churches. There are other approaches to the Bible that are similar to this, for example, the following through of a particular motif about liberation. It is an extremely important way to handle the Bible in one sense, but it also raises questions. How do we find the right balance between the 'grand sweep', this basic story, and the details of particular stories, including the ones that seem on occasions to fit very badly with the basic story? Sometimes, often without realising it, we prioritise the main thrust of the story and apparently twist the details of particular stories to fit it. So the image of God hardening the hearts of the people and thereby seeming to refuse them salvation, is reinterpreted as a statement wholly about human choices, without God having anything to do with it. (Look at how you might interpret Mark 4:11-12, for example, echoing Isaiah 6:9-10.)

This becomes important when it seems that stories which actually make women visible are often counted as stories that are incidental to the main plot. That might be the case with the stories about Hagar or Miriam, for example. To some extent women fit into the main biblical narrative in the same way as men do. Women and men are made by God (though with some questions left if you think the separate sexes have been made for very different purposes). Women and men are redeemed by God in Jesus. But in terms of named, active characters in the story, women are in the minority, sometimes invisible but assumed, following after, but occasionally highlighted as exemplary. When women do appear, it is usually in restricted roles, often because of their relationships to husband or children. In the past that has undoubtedly been used to argue that, therefore, women *should* be in particular roles.   Some Christian communities are still using the Bible in that way.

While on the one hand I know the necessity of working with assumptions about the one, single story which the Bible tells, and which is the focus of Christian proclamation, I also warm to other views of the Bible, which also inform my preaching. 'I think that we are beginning to see that the strength and power of the Bible is precisely that it is NOT clean and coherent; it is angular and disjointed, full of contradictions, ambiguous and fragmented.  In fact the Bible is a lot like life itself.'[9]  That allows all sorts of scope for exploration, for delving in the treasure chest.   But it necessarily involves dealing with aspects of the Bible which may need critique in the light of the main thrust of the story.  Gerd Theissen describes his approach to the Bible as both liberal with the text and bound by it.[10]   'Texts potentially have the power to transform . . .  If texts can gain such great power over human life, we should not accord just any texts this power over us.  The criterion is clear at one point: where texts have caused suffering we must interrupt their influence. Certainly we can understand such texts and make them comprehensible, but we should contradict them if we want to prevent them from influencing lives.'[11]  It is in ways like this that I, as a woman and a preacher, can put together both a deep love for the Bible, and a sense that, because it was written in patriarchal cultures, the Bible is also male-centred with occasional signs of outright misogyny.[12]

There are different practices among preachers with regard to use of the Bible and lectionaries.  Methodist preachers still exercise considerable freedom of choice over whether to use the recommended lectionary (currently the Revised Common Lectionary).  Some years ago in the United States, a lectionary was produced 'for women'.  It aimed to highlight passages that were 'good news' for women, and to provide a greater visibility for women within the Bible, so that women of today's society might more readily find the God who calls them, as women.   Lectionaries appear to guide us in what is appropriate for proclamation – and it is clear that the compilers of lectionaries no longer think that absolutely everything in the Bible lends itself to preaching.

A brief glance at the index to the lectionary we are currently using in the British Methodist Church suggests that changes have been underway in the last few years. Most of the major women characters of the Old Testament are featured (such as Miriam, Deborah, Ruth, Hannah, Esther) – at least in edited highlights. Since the gospels are read almost in full, gospel stories of women are told as well as of men. Where the continuous reading of Genesis is concerned, we might get the impression that women's stories are really those which are irrelevant to the main thread of 'the' story. We read some of Hagar and Sarah's stories, but much is left out about Lot's wife and daughters, Rachel and Leah, Dinah and Tamar, presumably because many of the 'minor' stories of the patriarchs are themselves left out.

Any preacher who has been preaching since at least the mid-1980s and who generally uses the lectionary will have acquired familiarity with three lectionaries. As an example of change, whereas on the Sunday given the theme 'The Family' in JLG1, two possible versions of the household codes were set (with the directive that wives should submit to their husbands), in JLG2 the household code in Ephesians was set once in the lectionary (for one of the four years), and RCL relegates its one passage (from Colossians) to a second service. That presumably reflects a shift among many denominations at the end of the 20th century as to the relative importance of certain biblical passages. Whether we use a lectionary or our own choices, we are always making decisions about the relative importance (the cultural relevance?) of various passages.

However, paying attention to the place and roles of women in the Bible does not mean that women preachers will preach only from restricted passages of the Bible (though sometimes this seems expected of them). I find myself caught in a neat cleft stick of my own making here, and can only tell my own story, with some hesitation. I have usually been in the practice of following the lectionary for my choice of readings, or at least starting with the lectionary readings. I have not deliberately chosen to preach 'about' women of the Bible, or to preach from passages with that focus alone, except in the case of one five-week series on the women in Jesus' genealogy according to Matthew 1 – and the suggestion for that series came first from the male colleague with whom I was leading worship. And yet the witness is that when I do preach on passages which touch this interest for me, there is a liberation about my preaching. That is my own feeling and it is affirmed by others! It is as if there is both a greater freedom and a stronger inspiration operating.

There are many ways of exploring what we are doing with the Bible when we preach and therefore how we see our role as preachers in relating to the Bible. We may be trying to tell the story the Bible tells in a straightforward way. We may see it as our source, our 'jumping off point', the beginning but not the end of our explorations in the proclamation of the gospel. We may see ourselves as bridging the gap between the pages of the Bible and the experiences of daily life. We may feel that the self-disclosure of God is witnessed to in the Bible in the images and thought forms of its day and that it is the role of preachers to reclothe the truths of the gospel in the language of our own day. We may feel, certainly on occasions, that it is necessary to disrupt the biblical text in some sense so that in unfamiliarity it might be seen afresh.

It may seem strange to some that I have come to the end of a chapter on the Bible, albeit a brief chapter, without mentioning the *authority* of the Bible. I believe authority is given as well as accepted. To recognise or accept the authority of a text is bound up with interpreting it in a way that has positive meaning for the community within which the interpreting takes place. Thus when the Bible conveys a message of freedom and healing it is authoritative. Where it is interpreted such as to limit and damage people, it is not.

# 4

# RELATING TO JESUS

The central and distinctive focus of Christian preaching
has from the beginning been Jesus. The disciples, after
Jesus' death and resurrection, told the story of Jesus.
Luke, as the writer of Acts, tells us that the core of those
sermons was the summaries the apostles told their
audiences of the significant facts of Jesus' life, death and
resurrection. Paul writes to the Corinthian Church: 'I did
not come proclaiming the mystery of God to you in lofty
words or wisdom. For I decided to know nothing among
you except Jesus Christ, and him crucified' (1 Cor 2:1-2).
Since, for Christians, Jesus embodies what it is most
significant that we know of God, that tradition of
proclaiming Christ is definitive of the Christian Church.
In order to exist, the Church must proclaim what God has
done for the world in and through Jesus of Nazareth, the
Christ.

## The preacher's spiritual life

I use again the structure of the last chapter by starting
with the preacher as Christian disciple, whose experiences
are interpreted first in that framework of Christian
discipleship which is shared with many others. A pre-
eminent strand in the Christian tradition has been the
calling of people into a personal relationship with God
through relationship with Jesus Christ. The gospel is
centred on a person, and, therefore, on a personal
relationship. The development of this relationship with
God in Christ is the spiritual life which all Christians

pursue, including preachers. There will, however, be as many different ways of construing that relationship as there are Christian disciples.

For myself, I must relate, in all relationships, as a human being and as a woman. The particulars that define me and my relationships to others in society include my sexuality (a term I am using here, inexactly, to include both my gender and my heterosexuality). Those facets of myself do not disappear suddenly in relating to God in Christ, although there are a variety of ways in which they may be understood or used. From her experience of spiritual direction, Kathleen Fischer[1] explores some of the images women have used to describe their relationship to Jesus. Some women, she finds, image that relationship in terms of male/female; some divert their attention from those physical and psychological differences by developing a relationship to Christ, the resurrected and ascended one, seen as now beyond gender. Some take biblical images, such as the 'I am' sayings from John's gospel, which do not have specific gender implications, and use them to image the spiritual relationship to God in Christ.

In Christian history, some mystics, both male and female, have explicitly used sexuality in their images of relationship with Jesus. Some male mystics have imagined themselves into female roles in that relationship – often into very stereotyped, passive, 'female' roles. On the other hand, there is also considerable recent work on Jesus *as a man* for present-day male disciples. 'The theological significance of Jesus is being interpreted in relation to many of the concerns of men which have found expression in the literature of men's studies. Jesus becomes a model for men's relations with women; he is understood to embody a male sexuality and a male intimacy which is perfect; . . . in Jesus men may find a new model for friendship.'[2] Perhaps that simply serves to emphasise women's need to recognise that relationship to Jesus is relationship between woman and man. It therefore has a particular element of difference, at least in terms of relating to the historical Jesus of Nazareth.

Where the gender issue also becomes important is in the relationship between the male Jesus of Nazareth, and the being of the trinitarian God. In relating to a male Jesus, are we relating to a male God? There are certainly preachers who are still giving the answer 'yes' to that, even though for many others it seems equally obvious that the God who created male and female 'in our own image' is beyond being captured within gender differentiation as human beings understand it. What, then, of the furore there still is at any attempt to image God as female in theological, and particularly in liturgical language? Usually this has been about addressing God as 'mother' (itself a limited image). The great unease expressed suggests to me that many have quite clearly already been relating to a gendered God, who is male. Imagery about a 'male' God has never created such horror – though it is just as close to idolatry. We need to be reminded that 'male' is no more neutral than 'female' – male images do not include both male and female. Attempts to change dominant metaphors have affected not just how we talk or think about God. They have affected the way in which we construe our *relation* to God. Difficulties in changing metaphors have revealed how much gender is *already* an aspect of our naming of God, and our relating to God; an aspect of our theology and our spirituality.

Prayer is the grammar of relationship with God. It is also the hidden and utterly essential precursor to preaching. So prayer, and the whole business of how we develop our relationship to God through Jesus needs to be given the preacher's attention. The preacher's gender is a more or less conscious factor in that relationship. For me, an exploration of prayer includes an exploration of the images through which I 'see' the God who is revealed in Jesus, and the kind of language that is comfortable for me to use in prayer and study. That language comes from a mixture of sources. I am relatively comfortable with the dominant tradition of 'father' imagery for God, and that is part of my prayer life, *alongside* psalms and prayers which refer to God as 'she'. Diversity of image and language is enriching for me in my relationship with God and that experience informs my preaching. So, for any preacher,

Jesus may be Lord, friend, companion, brother, lover, judge, teacher. I would suggest our preaching can only be enriched by our awareness of a diversity of images which express relationship to God through Christ, both because the diversity may enrich our own lives, and because those images that mean little to us personally may have powerful resonance to strengthen the spiritual lives of others.

## The Jesus of the gospels

This section 'straddles' two chapters, linking in to chapter 3, 'Relating to the Bible' as well as 'Relating to Jesus'. Without deviating too much into the paths of difficulty over the 'quest of the historical Jesus', it matters that I consider how preachers may react to the Jesus of the gospel records. In particular are there specific issues raised for some women preachers? Perhaps not, for there are many disciples, learners and preachers, both male and female who have been fascinated to look again at one aspect of the gospel records: namely Jesus in his relationships with women.

Some have wanted to claim Jesus as 'the first feminist' – a suggestion originally put forward by a man in an article in 1971.[3] This tends to mean focusing on the ways in which Jesus may have transgressed boundaries in his own society which should have kept such a public figure from having much to do with women. Thus, accepting the touch of a woman with 'an issue of blood' or touching the body of a young girl presumed to be dead are seen as violating taboos that kept religious men clean, both taboos about impurity and taboos about women. The danger of such arguments is that they depend on a demonising of the Jewish society at the time of Jesus on very little solid evidence. Even negative quotes by Jewish rabbis (usually of a period later than Jesus) could be countered with examples of women in relatively powerful positions, including those Jewish women who became leaders in Christian churches.[4] However, I still think it is possible to construe Jesus' relationships with women as remarkably close on evidence internal to the gospels, rather than on some idea that Christianity was far more enlightened than Second Temple Judaism in such matters.

For the writer of John's gospel, Jesus' attitude is occasion for comment – or at least questioning thought – by the disciples. In the story of Jesus and the Samaritan woman in John 4: 'Just then his disciples came. They were astonished that he was speaking with a woman . . .' (John 4:27). The later ending of Mark's gospel specifically reproves those who did not listen originally to the women's stories of resurrection: 'Later he appeared to the eleven themselves as they were sitting at the table; and he upbraided them for their lack of faith and stubbornness, because they had not believed those who saw him after he had risen' (Mark 16:14).

On the other hand, some people react negatively to attention given to Jesus and women in the gospels, arguing that it diminishes our attention to other more important aspects. Arguments are fought out over Jesus' valuing of women. The fact that there were clearly women who followed Jesus in his itinerant ministry is played off against the fact that the 12 closest disciples were all male. Healings of women are lined up against healings of men. It seems clear that Jesus had close friendships with some women, perhaps especially Mary of Magdala, and Mary and Martha of Bethany. In three of the gospels women have a particularly prominent role, over against men, in the stories of the passion and the resurrection of Jesus.

I am fascinated by the literary shaping of two stories in John's gospel, in chapters 3 and 4. At the beginning of chapter 3 we meet Nicodemus, a male teacher of Israel and council member, who comes to Jesus by night. He does not understand what Jesus is saying. He also fades from the story indistinguishably. Chapter 4 tells the story of a woman of Samaria, immoral by some standards, unlearned presumably, and probably unregarded in her town, who meets Jesus in the middle of the day. Jesus engages with her in conversation and, though she may not

41

fully understand, she certainly sticks with it. She is the recognised conversation partner throughout. She does not 'fade' from the story until she has become one of a number of figures in the gospel who are ideal witnesses, who bring other people to Jesus, which is the first step in enabling those others to develop their own relationship with Jesus. It is hard to imagine a more deliberate set of contrasts, or, therefore, a more positive picture of a woman enquirer over against a man. That comparison does seem to depend on an element of surprise that it should be the Samaritan woman and not Nicodemus who responds appropriately (though note which character is named). Presumably the surprise reflects the disciples' memories of Jesus. There is no need to highlight these instances over against what we imagine Judaism of the time to have been like: it is enough to see them over against later practices and attitudes in the Christian Church to see their radical nature.

These are aspects of interpreting the gospels with which preachers should be familiar. It is up to individual preachers to decide their relative importance. Preachers are constantly making choices as to what they highlight in the stories of the life of Jesus. Do we comment on his relationships with women in particular, or treat them in exactly the same way as Jesus' encounters with men? Do we echo the surprise evident in the gospels, remembering that the fact that it is there at all is a sign that the writers of the gospels recognise a weakness in the disciples which they are implicitly claiming not to share!

In the 1940s, Dorothy L Sayers noted the strangeness of Jesus in comparison to the Christian Church in a quotation which has achieved a wider audience through its use in the liturgical resource book *Celebrating Women*:

> Perhaps it is no wonder that women were first at the Cradle and last at the Cross. They had never known a man like this man – there has never been such another . . . There is no act, no sermon, no parable in the whole gospel that borrows its pungency from female

perversity; nobody could possibly guess from the words and deeds of Jesus that there was anything 'funny' about woman's nature.

But we might easily deduce it from his contemporaries, and from his prophets before him, and from his Church to this day. Women are not human; nobody shall persuade us that they are human; let them say what they like, we will not believe it, though One rose from the dead.[5]

Was Jesus a feminist? It is far too anachronistic a label to be used of Jesus in any meaningful sense. Mary Daly responded to Swidler's article (see note 3 above): 'The response that appears to be forthcoming from many women goes something like this: "Fine. Wonderful. But even if he wasn't, *I am*." '[6] Jesus certainly did not speak out against patriarchy in any way that would be recognisable today. Nor, if we take his historicity seriously, should we expect it.

It may be that for some women who are preachers, as for me, it matters to come to some conclusions as to how Jesus regarded and treated women, precisely because Christianity's record has been frequently poor, as well as at times good. It matters for me personally, in the way I relate to Jesus; it matters in the way I preach from the gospel material. It involves choices about parts of the Bible that may not always appear to be in line with each other. The words with which the writer of 1 Timothy silences women in Christian congregations are not attributed to Jesus. That is crucial for me, though it may raise many questions about the canon of the Bible for others.

There is another way in which preachers in particular may relate to the Jesus we find in the gospel texts. Jesus himself was a preacher. But it may not be immediately clear how that relates to today's preachers. In fact D W Cleverley Ford specifically distanced Christian preaching from the preaching of Christ, since Christian preaching presupposes the cross and resurrection. It is the proclamation that can only take place after the resurrection of Jesus.[7] Despite that objection, I am still drawn to the picture of Jesus as preacher. The attraction for me is in the invitational style of Jesus' preaching and teaching; in the unfinished parables which invite a response from the hearer, and yet which do not prescribe what that response will be. It is the encouragement to see God at work in the most ordinary things of life, and even if those most ordinary things are still usually imaged from the world of men, sometimes they are surprisingly imaged in female terms.

## Jesus as model

Jesus as preacher is only one way in which Christians may regard Jesus as a model for their lives now. That is not such an obvious relation as it might at first seem, since 20 centuries separate us from the circumstances and context of Jesus as a historical figure, and we have come to realise the extreme importance of context to every human life, which must include Jesus if his life was truly human. The truth is that there are strong strains of unorthodoxy in many Christians' views of Jesus, in which the divinity of Jesus is used in a way which 'transcends' his human limitations, and in which Jesus' humanity is, I would argue, actually diminished. That emphasis on divinity, though, also raises its own problems about how to regard Jesus as a model in any comprehensible way. Do we understand Jesus as unique, or as a representative human figure? Perhaps he is both, for us; but that answer doesn't solve the question of how he is to be a model for us; how Jesus is or is not normative for us. That matters to our preaching, for I imagine I am not the only one to use an argument in a sermon which runs (sometimes all too simplistically): Jesus behaved in such and such a way, and so should we.

The particular aspect of Jesus as model which has had great power over the centuries, but which many today are questioning, is the use of Jesus as a model of self-sacrifice. Jesus gave himself up for us; we should give ourselves up for others. We should put others' needs before our own. We are told in the gospels to deny ourselves. Any self-love is portrayed as the ultimate wickedness and a rebellion against God, part of the ultimate sin of pride. Despite this being a dominant discourse in Christian history, and in Christian preaching, it has been questioned in recent years.

Some have argued that this particular model of discipleship has been used to enforce gender patterns in which 'giving up' is seen more as the woman's part than the man's. It has certainly been used to critique women's aspirations to leadership, more stringently than men's. The danger is that a denial of self can in the end be a denial of life itself, and that some Christian discourses, in treating humans as worthless sinners, have denied a further Christian truth, that God loves us as we are. It is also arguable that we can come up with more rounded pictures of Jesus, which emphasise his strong sense of self and mission, his attention to his own needs for rest and quiet, and his choice not to sacrifice himself at the wrong times (see John 8:59).

Behind this questioning of a key strand of Christian tradition is the fear that the language of self-sacrifice is used to damage people. It has undoubtedly been used to keep people in relationships and in places which damage them, when they have little or no choice. I think we need to bring the place of choice firmly back into the picture. To use the example of Jesus to tell a woman that she must stay within a violent relationship, or to refuse people legitimacy for their opposition to injustice is to misuse the picture of Jesus as a model (normative) for us.

Another side to the use of Jesus as a model for us is that which comes from the biblical texts about our being transformed into the likeness of Christ. That raises questions about the ways in which women can reflect the likeness of a man. Is it that all of us are to be transformed into the likeness of a non-gendered image, in which our sex and our gender are irrelevant (putting us in danger of denying a fundamental part of our humanity)? Or is it, as some early Christian groups seem to have thought, that women should aspire to be like men in discipleship, and that the mark of 'successful' discipleship was to be called and treated as male? The first of those alternatives is more likely to appeal to modern Christians. Perhaps here we explicitly resort to an image of Jesus, popular from Jungian thought, as balancing masculine and feminine characteristics, and argue that that is the model for our transformation. The danger of that line of argument is that it still enshrines stereotypes of masculine and feminine, with the inherent likelihood that men and women will be expected in the end to conform to particular characteristics developed outside themselves.

## A male Saviour

The question has been asked in relatively recent years: 'Can a male saviour save women?' To some it will seem a nonsensical question, but it is not only a recent question. Various groups in Christian history, perhaps most notably the 18th century Shakers, have felt the need for a female saviour figure to 'balance' and 'complete' the male saviour, Jesus. Rosemary Radford Ruether asked the question in a form which has resonated with many others more recently.[8] In her investigation she argues that in one sense there is no argument since there has *never* been a suggestion in Christian tradition that men were saved rather than women, or even that women were more difficult to save (although it could be argued that there have been lines of thought which saw women as more in need of salvation than men, on account of being closer to the blameworthy Eve). The theology which underpins Ruether's view of salvation is one which emphasises the *humanity* of Christ over his maleness, and which does not ground Christ's work of salvation in his incarnation in a *male* body. In taking on a *human* form, Jesus lived and died and rose such as to bring about salvation. So there is no problem, no issue?

The problem comes in the shape of other theological themes which *do* rely on the maleness of Jesus in some particular way, and which have been used to exalt men as the stronger or superior sex over women. Some arguments arise from answering the question, to what extent is salvation complete now? How much of our 'fallenness' still remains in this world? To what extent does the salvation which we experience now change the world around us? Groups of Christians through the Church's history have argued over the extent to which salvation changes the orders of society. Early Quakers argued that the work of salvation included a radical change in relations between men and women. They therefore encouraged women in leadership, and guaranteed the persecution of Quakers by other Christians. 'High' views of Christian leadership as priesthood, and some 'low' views as well, have reflected the idea that it is more appropriate for men to be in leadership, either because that is set out in the orders of creation (though these only really become apparent – or are created? – as a result of the Fall), or because it is more appropriate for men to represent Christ because Christ was male. When does the maleness of Christ matter and when does it not?

Since 1974 when Edwina Sandys sculpted a female figure on a cross there have been several outbreaks of horror and outrage at such 'representations' of Christ. Teresa Berger, whose teaching career was blocked because she had mentioned 'a female Christ-child in the manger and a female figure on a cross',[9] questions why such strong outrage is expressed. After all, we have become used to images of Christ in the guise of many world cultures: a black Christ, a campesino Christ, an Asian Christ. These are not historically accurate representations, yet none of them is seen as questioning the historicity of the Christ-event. But when a female figure is substituted for a male figure, the outcry *does* centre on the fact that such a representation conflicts with the basic historicity of Jesus of Nazareth. Does the uproar actually suggest that gender is, in the end, a more foundational aspect of our perceptions of ourselves and other people than is ethnicity? (It will be interesting to see what reactions there are if images of 'the disabled God' gain ground – will they be judged in the same way as varying ethnic representations, or in the same way as varied gender images?) It also suggests that there is still a huge barrier to our seeing female figures as representative of Christ. Here is a limitation to our imagination of what incarnation is about. As preachers, can we point to a variety of images to show the ways in which Christ is incarnated in the world today, or do we confine the notion of incarnation to the limited period of the earthly life of Jesus of Nazareth, and thereby lose a rich vein of Christian tradition about Christ's life in the world now?

This chapter will look to many much more like a chapter on theology in general than a chapter on preaching. But it is our theology that informs our preaching. It is preachers' use of images about Jesus, our choice of stories to tell from his life, or about his death and resurrection, that aids or hinders the development of thinking and speaking about God within the Church. And how we think and speak about God affects the development of other people's relationship with God in and through Jesus Christ. If we are offering people images of Jesus which have relevance to their quest for hope and healing, for salvation and justice/righteousness, we will be helping to build up very different communities of faith from those that will emerge if we concentrate on images which aid the destruction and damage that some have identified within the Christian tradition.

# 5

# RELATING TO
# THE CHURCH

W e come to any examination of preaching in a context
where the vast majority of words heard from
pulpits, and other places of authorised preaching in the
Christian tradition have been the words of men.  It is
simply a historical fact.  The question here is to do with
the impact of that history on the present and the future.  In
this chapter I look briefly at some historical pointers, and
examine relating to the Church in the sense of relating to
the Church's historical tradition.  But I also try to examine
some of the stories that women who are preachers have
told me about their experience of preaching.   This
information has been gathered in a fairly unscientific way,
through a questionnaire in a very small-scale survey.  One
of the areas I am trying to pinpoint is the intuitions, stories
and odd comments overheard by women, and sometimes
by men, about women preachers.  It is this area that is so
often left unexamined.   So this chapter is necessarily
impressionistic, but its examples can still act as a stimulus
to further exploration of experiences that do or don't tally
with those mentioned here.

## Stereotypes about (and from) women preachers

In this short section, I concentrate most explicitly on
the perceptions of women preachers, looking at how some
women feel they are regarded in the Church.  So this
section goes wider than my own perspective, but is still

grounded in the issues I find in my relating to the Church. I used a questionnaire to ask the questions that fascinate me about how some women preachers think they are regarded, in a variety of Church denominations – though mainly Methodist. What was revealed was the stereotypes that some women preachers feel they are living with, not in society as a whole, but specifically in the Church. I have noted before that one of the mechanisms by which stereotypes work is that they induce the attitude that all women can be judged alike, rather than first and foremost as different individuals. There is the perceived burden that all women will be judged by my example, not if I do well and get it right, chiefly, but if I 'perform' badly. It is still the perception of some women, though, that their preaching is unwelcome simply because they are women: the suspicion that it is not the preaching, but the preacher-who-is-a-woman who is being judged. I hope, and believe, that this is less true in Methodist churches than others. One United Reformed Church ordinand witnesses, though: 'After I preached I overheard, "Very nice, but it should be a man."'

Many reported stereotypes centre on appearance and sound. Some women believe that comments are made about women's appearance more often than about men's, and ask what lies behind it. (Men who go beyond the bounds of sober suit-wearing, or whose ties or shoes are the subject of comment may disagree.) But there are valid questions to ask about whether women are more 'defined' by their appearance, expected to give more attention to their appearance than men, in modern Western societies. It seems clear that some in churches still worry about whether (particularly younger) women will be sober enough in dress. Comments on appearance tremble on the easily misinterpreted line between appreciating a compliment and feeling patronised. 'It's nice to have someone young and pretty in the pulpit' was one reported comment which left the hearer feeling patronised, with the impression that whatever she said would not have mattered. Similarly, whatever the best scientific evidence may say about the overlap in acoustic range between the voices of women and men, comments about women having soft voices, or screeching voices (oddly inconsistent!) abound. This seems a fairer matter of comment, in a speaking role, but is not necessarily objective. However, there's no denying that incidents that are important to some will not be to others. Marjorie Dobson comments in an article in *Worship Live*, 'Neither my gender, nor my age, seemed to be of concern to minister, fellow preachers or congregations. In fact, the only minor sensation I caused was by my absolute refusal to wear a hat in an era when it was still considered necessary for all women to do so in church. There were also one or two remarks about my three-inch stiletto-heeled shoes, but I had the ready excuse that I couldn't be seen over the edge of some of the larger pulpits unless I was wearing them.'[1]

What other stereotypes do some women feel are operating, alive and well, in present-day churches? There is the one that says a woman should preach on Mothering Sunday, and it could be any woman, as if all women understand about mothering issues. (I don't – I am not a mother, nor have I ever been in a position to be socialised into the care of young children.) There is the perception that women make good speakers at women's meetings, but not good preachers, borne either out of a sense of the unsuitability of women in pulpits, or out of a sense that women are not as forceful, or assertive, or do not carry conviction in the way that any man is expected to. Other kinds of stereotypes, or hinted generalisations, perhaps carry a whole range of different value systems: do women use a more conversational style, are they more anecdotal, do they contextualise and bring their sermons into contact with daily life more than men; do they use their families for illustration; do they use the imperative in sermons less than their male colleagues? I suspect all of us could drive a bus through these stereotypes with some reflection on the variety of preachers we have heard, women and men. What fascinates me is the persistence of the stereotypes and the sense that many preachers (perhaps both women and men) are feeling judged before they begin to lead worship, because of assumptions about their gender.

## The Christian tradition

In briefly discussing aspects of 'the Christian tradition', I am using one heading to stand for two areas of exploration. One aspect is the history of the Christian tradition, including the history of women's preaching. The other aspect is a reflection on the Christian tradition which preachers are particularly responsible for handing on. Perhaps, then, it is unfair to start with a work of fiction, but I do!

> He knew but two types of Methodist - the ecstatic and the bilious. But Dinah walked as simply as if she were going to market, and seemed as unconscious of her outward appearance as a little boy: there was no blush, no tremulousness, which said, 'I know you think me a pretty woman, too young to preach'; no casting up or down of the eyelids, no compression of the lips, no attitude of the arms, that said, 'But you must think of me as a saint.' She held no book in her ungloved hands, but let them hang down lightly crossed before her, as she stood and turned her grey eyes on the people. There was no keenness in the eyes; they seemed rather to be shedding love than making observations; they had the liquid look which tells that the mind is full of what it has to give out, rather than impressed by external objects.[2]

George Eliot's portrait of Dinah Morris, the gifted young preacher who submits at the end to the Wesleyan Conference's decision 'to forbid the women preaching',[3] is thought to be dependent on her Methodist aunt who was a preacher. It is a piece of fiction, drawn from observation of life, that reflects both the gifts of women who were called to preach at a particular period of history, and the controversy which surrounded them.

We can find examples of women preaching in public from all periods of the Christian Church. But they are almost always a focus of controversy, at least having to justify their position. Hildegard of Bingen, for instance, in the 12th century, began preaching in monastery chapters late in her life and occasionally in public. She took on that role, because she believed it was justified by her role as prophet (since she understood her 'visions' as prophetic messages). Examples of women prophets could be found in the Bible, so it was a role women could fulfil; it is even likely that she construed the calling of women as prophets, and of herself in particular, as an example of God using the weakest in the world to be his instruments.

In the 17th century, the Quakers were one group who took a stand for women's public ministry, including speaking/preaching. Margaret Fell argued in *Women's Speaking Justified, Proved and Allowed of by the Scriptures* (1667) that any prohibitions on women's preaching referred to women under the law, not to women under grace and the compulsion of the Holy Spirit. Her arguments remind us that there have been disagreements over the interpretation of biblical texts for a long time! In studies of other historical periods, too, there have been important rediscoveries about women's preaching, along with an acknowledgement that not everything can be recovered. So, to take just one instance, Bettye Collier-Thomas gives examples and analyses black women's preaching in America in the 19th and 20th centuries.[4]

Methodism, in particular, has had a varied history over women and preaching. In the evangelical revival of the 18th century in Britain, the urge to preach 'came not only to educated people but to the most unlikely and apparently ill-fitted, like soldiers or tradesmen or sometimes women'.[5] In her chapter in *Workaday Preachers*, Dorothy Graham tells the story of women local preachers. Wesley himself was clearly ambivalent about women as preachers, believing that preaching itself was outside their appointed sphere, yet they might be permitted to speak in more private meetings. But he acknowledged the ministries of women whose work he saw as clearly blessed by God. Though Wesley never appointed a woman as an itinerant preacher, several exercised such a ministry in all but name. Dorothy Graham's researches about the various Methodist groupings confirm that though there are examples in all of them of women preachers, local and itinerant, there were still controversies surrounding them. 'The whole question of women preaching was never very far from the minds of church authorities, especially as the Methodist connexions became more settled, respectable and conformist, which usually meant toning down more extreme practices such as fervent evangelism and female preaching.'[6]

All of this is history – what relevance or impact does it have now? Perhaps to most women who preach now, and to most men, it has no relevance at all. But such questions might be asked about the study of any aspect of history whatsoever. We tend to prefer looking to our history when we consider it positive. (Some members of other denominations find Methodism notorious for its remembering of its denominational history.) Some of us find a need to recognise our history also where it is not so positive, where it is a history of illiberalism and the confining or limiting of groups of people. That aspect too is relevant in understanding where we have come from, and why until recently there have been relatively few women preachers. It may also, therefore, illuminate why some of us still feel that we stand out. We should also live with the recognition that the history of the Christian Church is the reason why some have left the Church.

But there is another aspect to the phrase 'the Christian tradition' as it refers to the Christian story, and to the doctrines and order preserved and developed by the Church over the centuries as part of the Church's attempts to interpret the Christian story. One of the roles of the preacher is to be part of the process of handing on the Christian tradition. The metaphor of 'handing on' suggests that 'tradition' is an identifiable object passed unchanged from one generation to another, but in fact it is to some extent shaped anew as each generation and each culture tells the Christian story to its own world. Preachers in particular have the privilege of being in that role, proclaiming the Christian story in our own world. In fact that is far from a mechanical role: it is instead a creative process. This process keeps us in dialogue with the tradition of which we form a part. But some preachers, both women and men, have believed that the tradition as handed on to them has been harmful, and have felt the need to challenge and change it. This, too, has been happening for centuries in the formation of the Christian tradition. Just think of Martin Luther and the beginnings of the Reformation.

For some of us, the tradition that we are part of and which we are to pass on, as well as to shape, seems a profoundly male-centred tradition, in which men are the prominent figures, in which women have been severely limited, and in which the very image of God, in whose image male and female are made, has been restricted too narrowly into 'masculine' categories. That introduces tensions into the heart of decisions to be made about preaching. Christine Smith, in a book on feminist preaching suggests, 'Even though many women at times fantasise about leaving the Christian tradition, many of us also know that to absent ourselves from it is to leave it unchanged.'[7] That may sound a threatening or dangerous position to those who don't believe that anything needs to be changed. But all preachers experience these tensions in some form or other in the struggle to see how their own understanding of Christian theology relates to other understandings to which the Christian tradition bears witness. Then they must further relate that to those who listen to their preaching. I am suggesting that the situation I highlight is just one variation of a much deeper struggle with which all of us who preach must engage.

For some, conflicts with the tradition become especially sharp in issues of inclusive language and imagery about God. I have tackled the subject of imagery about God already in chapter 4 in relation to personal spirituality, so I return to it here only as it affects the leading of public worship. There is no mileage at all in any stereotypes which suggest women have particular views on inclusive language and imagery: there is plenty of empirical evidence that women and men demonstrate a whole range of views. Some women feel (as I do) that it is crucial to our Christian development that we cease to address women with male terms, and that we widen the range of the images we use for God. Some women are hostile to any attempts to change language used about God, or about people, seeing it either as destructive or simply unnecessary; disputes among men would parallel these. Preachers will be found in both categories. There are also many shades of differing practice among those who think some of the traditional gendered language we use in churches needs reshaping.

For myself, I will not use language about people that refers to 'all' under male terms (man, men, mankind). I compromise when it comes to some traditional hymns, though people know that I will change the wording *I* sing (where I can) to something inclusive. When it comes to Bible readings, I may be happy to change such terms in the readings I read, but I am well aware others feel that is 'tampering' with the Bible. In the church where I minister currently, the answer is relatively simple. Since the pew Bible we use is the New International Version, I simply ask readers to read from the NIV inclusive language edition. When it comes to language about God, I am what many would regard as much more conservative. I try to use a range of images in prayer language addressed to God; 'Father' will often be one of the images used, non-gendered images are frequent, but 'Mother' very rare. Although I would rather avoid gendered pronouns in speaking about God (for instance in sermons), where I do use a pronoun it will be 'he' rather than 'she'. The language preachers use is a matter of *choice*: I simply hope that the choice will be conscious and thought through rather than assumed.

## Accreditation and authority

Within Methodist structures, there is no problem at all about giving women authority to preach through the same system of training and accreditation as men. Since accreditation is the process by which women and men are given authority to preach on behalf of the whole

Methodist Church, women as well as men are part of the structures of authority within the Church. One aspect of accreditation, and part of the business of preachers relating to the Church is their relating to other preachers. All those who preach listened to preaching before they preached themselves. For most of us, other preachers will have been role models for us in some way. Sometimes that is a product of 'the system' in that, within Methodism, preachers have supervisors or mentors to help them in the development of their preaching. At best, people learn from each other, and develop their own voice. At worst, preachers in training are expected to conform to the styles of preaching preferred and practised by experienced preachers. For some 'on trial' this will always be a source of conflict, with the suspicion that they are being encouraged into another preacher's style of preaching, and not given sufficient help in developing their own. I wonder if some have experience of how this conflict can be overlaid by gender issues, for some women have felt they were being encouraged into styles more appropriate for men. To what extent is gender taken into account in your experience in the mentoring of local preachers?

Since women are given authority to preach, Methodism has effectively decided that the injunctions in 1 Timothy 2:11, refusing women authority over men, were relevant to a particular context, and not to all times and places, or else that they were never meant to be about preaching (though that seems unlikely). Almost any book on preaching has a discussion of authority somewhere. Whose authority is involved in preaching? Few would question that such authority must be understood as God-given at some point. Expanding on that, authority to preach comes from the Spirit; it is grounded in the work of God in the preacher and in the hearers, through the Bible and through the self-disclosure of God in the present. Some chiefly emphasise the authority of the preacher grounded in the Bible as God's authoritative word. Some would point to the authority I mentioned above, given by the Church through processes of training and accreditation.

D W Cleverley Ford argues that preaching is such a particular form of communication and authority because it is proclamation through a person. Therefore, he emphasises that aspect of the preacher's authority which is personal. That, in turn, gives him reason to note the huge dangers that go with the use, and potential abuse, of that kind of authority. Perhaps that is the perspective most easily missed if we keep the discussion in the area of the givenness of God's authority. It is worth at least noting here the lack of clarity in any distinction between the authority of the preacher and the authority in their preaching. In talking with one group of preachers about role models in their preaching, it was clear that they remembered people and their general styles, rather than particular sermons or even the general thrust of the content of preaching, so it was the preacher as much as the preaching which had authority for them. Perhaps the two spheres of authority cannot be entirely divorced from each other.

Any discussion on the authority of preaching now has to take place within a society, and, from my perspective, within an age-group, where 'authority' as a whole is a problematic concept. This is a significant area for the Church to address precisely because congregations are often made up of those whose notions of authority were formed in very different contexts. *I* assume that it is right and proper to demand that those in authority justify themselves and their pronouncements, and I put that down, to some extent, to a system of education that has taught me to ask questions and has tried to instil some criteria for judgement. I have been formed and socialised at a time when certain forms of authority are judged more harshly than others, particularly that authority which has become synonymous with domination – where 'authority' means 'authority over' people used to persuade to one's own point of view at best, used to stifle all questions and all opposition at worst. Different responses to different kinds of authority are evident in the Church, where at the extremes some want to question everything they are 'told', while others seek relatively safe and easy answers to all questions.

Both women and men who preach need to engage with questions of their authority in the Church in similar ways, within our current pluralistic cultural context. But preachers will come to the questions from very different places. Some will have lived through periods where women were not often seen in public positions of authority. Most who are preaching now will have some opinion as to the premiership of Margaret Thatcher and what that did, for better or worse, for the association of women and authority! In this context, it would be interesting to reflect on whether the pulpit has actually been regarded as a public space or a private space. I suspect it has been public enough from the point of view of the Church to explain why women have often been unwelcome in it. From the point of view of society, it may well seem much more private, so that the 'public' speaking of women within churches has not been much noticed in society.

So where might problems with authority have their impact for me as a preacher and a woman? Some women find themselves criticised (implicitly or explicitly) for not having the 'authoritative' style of men; some find themselves accused of aping men if they are seen to be inappropriately forceful. I am tempted on occasions to think that any measure of assertiveness in women is read as inappropriate force! The problems for me have much more to do with what model of authority I am seeking to use in preaching, and I think similar questions apply in that regard to personal and scriptural authority, because ultimately these are questions about how we see God relating to us. One Christian's image of God is essentially that of the one who must be obeyed, whose authority is imposed, who simply demands response in the framework of a predetermined plan. For another, God is one who allows us choices and space, for whom there isn't just a right and a wrong way, but who negotiates with us, who creates a dialogue with us, as a consequence of creating us with real freedom. Perhaps both portraits are overdrawn. But I think there is a significant distinction to be addressed. I want to move away from models of authority that imply domination, hierarchy, and perhaps even persuasion. They are the models often projected (though I think wrongly) by a model of preaching which sees the sermon as occasion for a monologue. If preaching, on the other hand, is more properly seen as dialogue (whether one voice is actually spoken out loud in that dialogue or not), we are in the area of questioning and creativity as the process by which we discern God's truth. This will be taken up again in chapter 6.

## The feminisation of the Church

Some time ago (I believe in 1995 or 1996) results of two surveys of the gender, ethnicity, age and educational background of, first, Scottish, then, English Methodist preachers were discussed in the LPMA magazine and in the *Methodist Recorder*. The surveys revealed that preachers were mainly white, middle-class and well-educated. They revealed that the majority of preachers were men, but also that it was possible to draw up projections for the future, on the basis of trends among preachers in training over the last few years, in which the majority of local preachers were female. The numbers of women taking up local preaching in Methodism had been rapidly increasing.

For some these projections sounded alarm bells. A clear inference was drawn that if there was a majority of women preachers, this would lead to an even greater drop in the number of men attending churches. Not only would women be in the majority in our congregations, but also in even more ministries (to go along with such areas already as Sunday school teaching). I simply comment that the fears expressed at the prospect of a majority of preachers being women are never paralleled with horror at a majority of male preachers. Nor is it usually commented on that the so far majority of men in our pulpits have presided over the period when it is asserted less and less men have been attending church. Nor is it apparently noticed that there has never been a period in the Church's history when women have not been in the majority in worshipping congregations. Women have often been the ones keeping churches going: a perhaps unrecognised leadership role. I don't suggest that this phenomenon is something to be ignored or applauded; simply that there is no evidence that more women in leadership roles of various sorts in the Church will automatically make things worse. These arguments are, of course, used with even more force when the ordination of women is under discussion. I found it interesting that the same arguments were being used in a Methodist context to do with women as preachers.

How, then, might some women feel about the Church that many have worked so hard to build, when some appear so anxious about their preaching, if not their presence? As a woman, various congregations within the British Methodist Church have provided me with the encouragement and space I have needed to build confidence as a Christian, and as a preacher. I have also had experiences of churches which have left me hurt and angry, particularly when the validity of my experience has been questioned. It seems to me we are still hugely split in the Church between those who believe the Church has not even begun to tackle issues about how men and women relate to each other in society and in the Church, and others who are fed up with what they think of as special pleading on behalf of a few women who are not badly off, but never seem satisfied. What the future holds may depend on whether we can explore these differences honestly and work with them.

# 6

# A VISION
# FOR PREACHING

In one sense, it is very simple to give a definition of preaching. Preaching, one might say, is the proclamation of God's truth, revealed in Jesus, the Christ. But that statement is not, for me, simple at all. It says nothing about the person doing the proclaiming, or the people to whom the proclamation is presented. I even want to think through the associations of the word 'proclamation'. Nor is 'God's truth, revealed in Jesus, the Christ' a simple matter. The various forms of Christianity that have existed over two millennia are abundant proof of the many ways in which that phrase has been understood, because of the many ways in which it can be, and has been *contextualised*. My understanding about God is not based on believing that I have a simplistic access to God's absolute truth. Instead, I believe in the necessity of searching, working towards an understanding of the revelation of God in Jesus, and working towards it not on my own but with others. Furthermore it has to include the possibility of my being wrong! Rather than something simple, preaching bears witness to a constant, enriching search and struggle to live towards God's truth, in our particular place. This is not to be construed, however, as always an intellectual search: it encompasses many other aspects of ourselves as well.

So preaching is not easy to define, or to envision. In the final section of chapter 1 I pointed briefly to a number of partial definitions which have informed what I think I am trying to do when I preach. The word 'proclamation' did appear there, when the deeds of God in the past, God's presence with us now and the calling forth of our response are announced in the community of faith. In that chapter I picked up the importance of the preacher's individuality, used and transcended by God's action, and have proceeded in the following chapters on that licence of personal perspective, hoping that it is being transcended in interaction with many readers. In chapter 1, preaching was also seen as creating opportunities for people to enter into dialogue with God, and to articulate an alternative world-view from that which is created in other places in our society. Yet added together these pointers do not make a neat and tidy definition of any sort.

This book has been about reflection on what we do in preaching week by week, fulfilling preaching appointments quarter by quarter. Frequently I have taken several steps back from the practice of preaching, and encouraged readers to do the same from their own points of view. What I intend to do in this final chapter is to articulate a vision of preaching, or aspects of a vision of preaching in this brief space, building on the hints of previous chapters. I concentrate on aspects of what I hope preaching can be in relation to who the preacher is, what preachers do in practice, and what I think is happening in preaching, particularly what God does in and through preaching. The section 'Preaching and experience' picks up material mainly from chapters 1, 2 and 5; the following section picks up on chapters 3 and 4 in particular. In both, I work one step further on with the implications of the material for our understanding and practice of preaching. The final few paragraphs affirm my hope in the activity of preaching, with a possible image for preaching which might take exploration further still. The chapter is therefore presented as a challenge to other preachers to examine what you do, what it reveals about yourself, and what it says about God, linking that firmly to the vision of preaching that speaks of where you want your preaching to go.

## Preaching and experience

The first five chapters of this book were reflections on my interactions with a series of contexts within which preaching takes place, all of which affect our perspective and our experience of ourselves, the world and God. The fact that preaching takes place in context, in fact within a whole range of contexts, is crucial in developing any vision at all that might express our ideals about the why, what and how of preaching. I believe that preaching becomes more valuable the more conscious we become of the effects of context upon us and of our ability to shape the environment in which we live. An incarnational faith demands that we take such things seriously. If preaching is said to be 'truth through personality' it is truth through the personality that has been built up through our varied experiences, and through the ways in which we have explored those experiences. That makes explicit the important idea that 'experience' is never straightforward; it is always mediated through our understanding and needs to be the focus of reflection at every point in our lives. This is particularly important when our experiences are explored as the vehicle of God's interaction with us, and offered as a possible model for God's interaction with others.

To give an example: we are becoming increasingly aware of how much a person's human experiences may shape their image of God, and, therefore, actually their experience of God. So the child who was told she would be loved only if she was good, or the child who was shown that the only important thing in life was his success, and that he must beat others to the top, may have, in adulthood, warped understandings of God's unconditional love. Only careful reflection on those experiences, the image of God that has been shaped by them, and other people's different experiences, understandings, even readings of the Bible will help to re-shape their relationship with God.

Perhaps it needs stating less in the Methodist Church than within some denominations, but, at a basic level, if women as well as men are preachers, a greater range of experiences is reflected in the preaching that takes place in our churches. This is all too often caricatured as women talking about babies, or the fact that only women can help us to reflect on childbirth. Actually I have heard more fathers, and particularly grandfathers, talking about babies in the pulpit than mothers or grandmothers! This is about what I termed in chapter 2 'voicing gender-specific experiences in preaching', even though I expressed discomfort about the ways in which stereotypes might still be projected in this way. I believe that women and men live with different sets of stereotypes projecting who they ought to be, what they ought to be interested in and how they should behave. We all face expectations, even pressures about what it is to be a human being, and about what it is to be a woman or a man. One of the issues about such social pressures is that being 'a man' is meant to be so distinct from being a woman. So expectations about appearance, about earning potential, about relation to paid work, and about social activities are still gender-specific to some extent. Only having acknowledged that can we say also that individuals notice such social pressures and respond to them in a whole variety of ways.

Preaching needs to reflect a wide range of experiences so that we are enabled as Christians to reflect on a myriad of ways in which God touches people's lives. We are to hear many stories, and out of those stories to learn something of the variety of God's ways with people. Here is the process I think takes place: people shape and explain their experiences by telling stories, *telling* their lives to themselves and others. Reflection on those stories within communities of faith leads to a naming of the ways in which God has been experienced. 'Story-telling' is just one name for that part of preaching which enables the truths of God to be connected with or found in human experiences. 'Story-telling' sometimes comes in the form of illustrations. It is the way to make the general more particular. We need many stories: biblical stories, stories of saints and sinners, first-century, 21st century and everything in between. They are not the 'add-ons', the necessary pauses for breath, the rhetorical flourishes, but the part of preaching that enables the congregation to recognise the ways in which what is spoken may connect with the ways they interpret their own experience and recognise or fail to recognise God in it. Donald English expected preaching to help people to identify and interpret what they experience, so that they can see in it the signs of God at work.[1]

Stories of human experiences, then, do two things for a vision of preaching. Firstly they are the way to acknowledge human diversity. They should be the way to undermine falsely universal language and challenge bland stereotypes. They must be true to varied human experience. The second thing that stories enable us to do is to name God. So the explicit naming of women's experiences within preaching enables God to be named out of female experiences, out of the ways in which women as well as men have encountered God. Sometimes that naming will sound exactly the same as the ways in which God has been named for centuries in the predominant traditions of the Church. Thus, some women will name God most powerfully, and with most honesty to their own experience, as 'Father', 'King', 'Lord', as 'Victim' and 'Priest', as 'Conqueror' and 'Saviour'. Sometimes that naming will sound radically new, and sometimes we will find themes picked up from traditions centuries old. Thus God may also be named, with similar metaphorical appropriateness and inappropriateness, with similar truth and a similar missing of the mark, as 'Mother', 'Midwife', 'Nurturer', 'Nurse', 'Lover', 'Companion', the One who gives birth to creation. Thus, also, God may be 'she' to us with as much accuracy and inaccuracy as God is 'he'.

But this assumes that we have stories to tell. It means that, in preparation for preaching, the preacher must be first and foremost a listener. Stereotypes are based on the assumption that others' experience is like one's own, or that a whole group of people can be lumped together in their attitudes, expectations and behaviour; stereotypes exist for just as long as we refuse to listen to people's stories. The preacher as listener *finds out* which experiences are shared and which aren't, by listening, rather than making assumptions. As soon as we make fully explicit the way in which other voices must contribute to 'my' preaching, we begin to glimpse one of the ways in which preaching, far from being a monologue, is actually *a communal event*.

I see this illustrated most vividly in ways many local preachers may not experience in their own practice of preaching, although as members of congregations and bereaved families they may see this. I am most acutely aware of the voices of others when I preach at a funeral service. The sermon for such a service has to be, for me, a combination of reflection on a particular life, and reflection on the truths of God in Christ, I hope as illustrated in that particular life. In preparation, there is the time spent with the bereaved family, planning the service and listening as carefully as I can to their stories about the deceased family member. People respond most positively, I have found, to a funeral sermon in which they can hear their own voices and their own stories echoed, and yet in which there is something more: as if it must be shaped by someone else, or put together with additional reflection, particularly theological reflection. I suggest that is actually a good model for all preaching.

It is a model that emphasises that preaching emerges from relationship, from connection with people, and from communities. I have explored in other chapters the ways in which preachers are formed within particular locations in society, within church traditions and so on. Every preacher emerges from a community and needs to be aware of that dimension of their own being, as well as the effect it has on preaching. All this is true of 'traditional' preaching, however much it sounds like a monologue. But there may be ways in which we can and should allow congregations to become even more aware of the communal aspect of the doing and hearing of preaching. If sermon-making is participative, or if the delivery of a sermon is constructed more explicitly as dialogue, or conversation, then we are simply becoming more aware of what is already going on. If we encourage questions and comment, either as part of the sermon, or immediately afterwards, or through appraisal of sermons, or house-group discussion in the few days following, preaching is more clearly communal. However, that kind of participation, I would argue, is going on silently all the time anyway, and that is right and proper. It emerges out of the right rooting of preaching in experiences, and it also encourages the critical faculties of the congregation to be used in the service of faith. From reflection on our own experiences and the experiences of others, we are brought to an understanding of the way in which preaching can be a communal event, relevant to the many individuals who make up the community of faith within which any act of preaching takes place.

One further aspect of experience that I want to make explicit is that preaching is an embodied act. I remember a local preacher on trial explaining graphically to me her understanding of preaching. She used gestures to *show* what preaching was to her: touching her chest/heart area she talked of connecting 'what's in here . . . with the Bible', laying her hand firmly on the Bible at her side, 'and with the experience of the people' and her hand swept a huge gesture in front of her as she watched the imaginary congregation, and as she metaphorically opened herself up to them. The final gesture said so much about her eagerness to interact with the congregations for whom she led worship, but she was someone who also always found leading worship a struggle. The phraseology was simple, yet the bodily showing of it had a power beyond the phrases as well. She was a preacher singularly conscious of embodiment in her preaching. She knew too that the creation of words is very much a part of our embodiment, but far from the only part.

The truth of women's preaching emerges from each woman preacher's living out of her human experience and her specifically female embodiment, as the truth of men's preaching also includes the bodily experiences of being male. This aspect of preaching is often reduced to a discussion of the gestures that a preacher uses. Further still it is reduced to the question of whether the preacher uses 'any distracting mannerisms'. In the pulpit, we do, though, have to remember that we communicate with our bodies, not simply with disembodied words. In fact 'in the pulpit' begs a question, since one of the questions about our bodies in preaching is where we actually are in the church when we preach. Beyond the church context, attention to embodiment, to incarnation, means attention to our body's strengths and vulnerabilities, to the requirements of our bodies (significantly different between some women and some men), the particular ways in which our bodies may break down. Even our awareness of God must happen as part of embodiment. This might lead us to new ways of thinking about incarnation and God's embodiment. How that experience comes to consciousness and is used will differ with each individual. The importance of embodiment is reflected in what appears to be a common experience of forgetting the words of a preacher, but remembering and being particularly affected by the manner, the posture, the tone of the preacher. It may be 'dignity', or 'an aura of holiness' or 'assertiveness' or 'aggression' that is remembered, but it becomes clear again that the preacher herself or himself is part of the message, as interpreted by the congregation.

My vision of preaching as it has emerged in this section is of preaching as a communal event, arising out of reflection on experiences. If, as preachers, we can encourage a variety of ways for people to participate in the preaching event, we will enhance our own and the congregation's awareness of that. My vision of *preaching* here has also proved to be very strongly a vision of the *preacher*. The 'ideal' preacher is one who is fascinated enough by the world, by people and by God to keep exploring, to keep on deepening her or his own experience through listening to and sharing the stories of others, including quite deliberately those who are very different from themselves. The preacher then works on articulating how the God who is found in those experiences can be named deeply and engagingly.

## Preaching expressive of God

In chapter 4 I used the theme of the preacher's spiritual relationship with God in Christ to ask questions about how the content and the language of our preaching expresses our beliefs about God. Here I build on that, and also give particular attention to the way in which I would hope what we believe about God influences the way in which we preach. What we say about God when we preach has to resonate with real images of God which are derived both from the Bible and from the way in which we find God working in the world around us. Some hopes for that kind of preaching were explored in the last section. But the manner of our preaching must be similarly theologically consistent.

The God who creates, who gives us the gift of ourselves and this world day by day, is the God also who seeks self-disclosure. God is *revealed* in the world and in Christ. The God who seeks self-disclosure also seeks relationship with that which is created. But God's revelation takes place in and through the messiness of real life, because even if we talk of the Bible as God's revelation, we read that, work with it and seek to 'apply' it in the contexts we are part of. It is this God who creates and reveals, of whom I am conscious in my study on those occasions when it feels as if what I am to preach has been *given* to me relatively easily, from beyond myself. But it is the same God at work when I struggle to wrest some meaning from the Bible which will speak to the congregation who hear *my* words first and foremost. God has often been found in obscurity, hidden even, and I at least experience the God who appears surprisingly, who does not always conform to my expectations (or even my theology). Here is the tension between the hiddenness of God and the revelation of God, which the Christian tradition has explored from its beginnings.

God is a risk-taker. God is revealed in the risky business of the birth of a child in poor circumstances; the incarnate God is vulnerable, and in the Christ-child is pictured for us as the God who chooses to be dependent on us, at least in part, as well as the God who lives with us in all the risks of our own lives. The risk-taking God is not a God who forces or compels us, who is so all-powerful that we are given no choice but to submit. With God there is always a choice.

God has to be a risk-taker for preaching to make any sense. Preaching seems to me one of the most risky methods God uses in self-disclosure and in working out the purposes of creation and salvation. It is surely an amazing instance of God vesting trust in people. I certainly don't believe that the whole of what goes on in preaching is our work, but a large proportion of it certainly is, and God's risk is that we could get it wrong. We could obscure God's activity instead of pointing to it. But it is a risk consistent with the part we are given in God's activity in the world. If you share with me some of those beliefs about what God is like, then it has implications both for the content of our preaching and for how we go about preaching.

Many textbooks and many preachers talk of preaching to persuade, or to convict and convince. Sometimes our terminology smacks of manipulation. But conviction can never be forced, and our methods must never make it look as if people have no choice. Proclamation of the gospel always leaves room for its rejection. But it also leaves room for exploration, so that people may be able to respond in the way that is right for them, not for us. Let me give an example of how this affects the content of preaching: one of the issues at stake in how we interpret the miracles of Jesus as told in the gospels is whether God puts us in a place where belief is forced. Were the 'miracles' so obvious that no one could be there and not see what happened? The gospels tell stories of people's confusion. With healings in particular (with which the people might well have been familiar from the presence of other healers around the time of Jesus), the question of belief usually has to do with whether people grasp the underlying meaning of Jesus' action. With the 'nature miracles', some modern interpretations have wanted to leave room for people to question what actually took place as well as what it meant. Those interpretations raise the question of whether 'miracles' force belief, or leave room for disbelief. Perhaps they can only be the inspirers of faith if they leave room for doubt. Questions about how God works become questions about how we interpret the Bible, and, therefore, inform the content of our preaching. But they must inform the manner of preaching also. The two need to be consistent with each other, and consistent with our own experiences of God. Preaching which offers various possible responses, which makes quite deliberate space for people's choices (even when we are quite sure what choices they ought to make) is preaching which is shaped by our experience of God's action.

We often talk about the 'power' of preaching. Sometimes the phrase is used to refer to the way in which preaching has certain effects upon people, sometimes it seems to refer to the rhetorical manner of preaching. 'Power', I would argue, is a very gendered concept in most cultures, although the precise contours of that in any particular culture take a lot of exploring. For my purpose here, the power of preaching must reflect the power of God. So it is the power of the child in the manger, the power of the healer, the power of the one confronting authority, and the power of the defeated one on the cross. It is only then, also, the power of the one who overcame death. God was expressed most clearly in Christ, in human embodiment and in vulnerability. The one who could perform wonders could be ignored and could be defeated.

In preaching, by methods which express something of God, our vulnerability, our weakness, our embodiment all become central. Something of this comes through whenever we recognise our own inadequacies as preachers. We experience it in our surprise at the unexpectedly clear 'results' of our preaching, which sometimes seem to bear little relation to our own uncertainties, weaknesses or purposes. I knew it in the wry complaint from a woman who said she had had to empty her purse into the collection plate after I had preached on one occasion, or when someone told me of a letter she had written to heal a relationship which had gone wrong long ago. They were reactions that both had connection with something I had taken part in, but also went way beyond anything in me. But we know it also in the many times in which we do not see the 'results' of our preaching. This is not somehow to oppose our weakness and God's power which works in spite of us. It is precisely in our weakness and in our embodiment that God is enabled to work. God works in the risky, vulnerable activity of our preaching.

I am fascinated by the number of people in our churches, despite the shifts in liturgical emphasis in the last 30 or so years, who still see the sermon as the most important part of any gathering for worship. I imagine that understanding was created by what churches (especially Protestant churches) said about God. God was revealed as the Word: the One who *spoke* creation into being is the One who came to us in Christ. Thus words have come to be seen as expressive of God *par excellence*. That is a theology which expects God to be in preaching by 'speaking' to our minds and hearts through human words. I would want to challenge the pre-eminence of that model and put it alongside others. God is Word, but also Light, Fire, Wisdom, Love, and so much more.

Preaching, and certainly the way preaching is placed within the whole context of worship, could offer models of God's action in relation to individuals and to the world as a whole other than God 'speaking'. Even our words can be the vehicle into other forms of experience. Silent or music-filled space for reflection may enable people to touch emotional realms not always accessed or expressed by words alone. Our preached words must, it seems to me, point towards action – liturgical action or the actions members of the congregation might take outside the liturgical space. Participation of others in the preparation or activity of preaching, as in other aspects of the worship, enables people to experience God accepting and using them. An emphasis on imagery in preaching – even images expressed verbally – can help people to connect to a sensory, physical world.[2]   These are a few, perhaps random ways, in which preaching might be an expression of the whole person to the whole person, since that is what God has both made and redeemed; ways in which the manner of our preaching might expand our horizons with regard to who God is and who we are as God's creation.

I have stressed above the extent to which preaching is a communal event.  Despite some of the shifts of the 1980s and 1990s, we arrive in the 21st century, at least in Western Christianity, with a strong sense of God dealing with individuals and a very limited sense of the God who deals with communities.  But God dealing with people corporately is also a strong biblical theme, which we can highlight in a way which still allows for the personal relationship between God and the believer.  We believe in a God who creates community, bringing individuals into a realisation of their interdependence where that has become weak, always building up the body of Christ.  The very act of preaching which takes place in communities, with the purpose of building communities is an expression of God's purposes.  The more that preaching can be experienced as a communal event, not just in the shared experience of listening, but in shared experiences of testing, weighing and learning, the better it will contribute to God's purposes of building community.  That purpose is furthered if we realise that community is *only* built where there is diversity, and even where people meet not in spite of their differences but because of them.  Does our practice of preaching cover up differences by expressing only that which we share, or by creating a false 'harmony' that never challenges any of our differences?  Preaching could be a better expression of community, even of the community which is the trinitarian God, where it allows for what is distinctive and different among the body of Christ.

One of the characteristics of Jesus' ministry was his invitation to all people to share in God's goodness and God's salvation.  The surprise of that in particular was that he invited those nobody else bothered to invite.  In that sense we would say that Jesus shows a God who is inclusive. 'Inclusiveness' is also a theme with which many people try to reflect on where we are in 21ˢᵗ century Britain's myriad of contexts and overlapping communities. Are the poor included or excluded? Are black and Asian people included or excluded? In what ways are women still marginalised in areas of social and economic life? How might disabled people be fully enabled by being more fully included in areas of life from which they have hitherto been barred? Much of this reflection is unfortunately tarred with the now disparaging term 'political correctness'. But our reflection on our society can be brought into parallel with reflection about God through the picture of Jesus' practice of broad table-fellowship, or through the early Church's realisation that they were called to break the bounds of the Jewish faith in inviting the Gentiles also into their relationship with God.

Yet we may be in danger of using the word 'inclusiveness' as a blanket, which can warm, but can also suffocate. Jesus not only invited people, he watched when they would not respond to the invitation. Jesus not only endeavoured to bring people into God's kingdom, he delineated powerfully the reasons people would be shut out, by exploring the kind of values and behaviour that had no place there. 'Inclusiveness' is not total.

How are these pictures of God reflected in the content and manner of preaching? I have already explored the notion that we need to include a greater variety of stories and experiences than our own or those similar to our own in preaching. Preaching is expressive of God when, through those stories, it links to where people really are so that they truly feel invited to share in God's salvation. I also find an analogy of this in my own method of preaching. As I prepare a sermon, I work by synthesis rather than division. I work by seeking connections between often disparate ideas (though not connections which dissolve difference). Sometimes that's about finding surprising connections between different biblical passages. Sometimes it's about the whole task of connecting biblical concepts with everyday life in the 21ˢᵗ century. The work of synthesis and making connections is a kind of inclusiveness.

But preaching is not just this. The pulpit is not a 'free speech' platform. In the end we are inclusive only of what reflects the gospel of Jesus Christ for us. Preaching which reflects God's kind of inclusiveness points to God's all-embracing love, but also points to that which is against God's love, showing the paths that lead away from God as well as the ones that lead towards God. The trouble, of course, is that we do not agree what constitutes those paths. It is one of the many areas in which our preaching must explore, and be tested, rather than expressing only our own prejudices. A similar point is made by saying that preaching must take sides – the sides which God takes in offering the good news in Christ to the poor and the sick and the sinful, resisting the machinations of the powerful of the world. The hard edge of prophetic challenge must, then, be evident in our preaching, showing up the aspects of our life and culture which make no easy 'fit' with the gospel. That, for me, is added to a necessary 'hermeneutics of suspicion', which asks hard questions about the traditions of the Church, and about some of the ways in which Christian faith has been expressed in past years and past centuries. There are things from Christian tradition I would want to exclude in the name of a credible, living faith for today, not least its devaluing of women. Then the preaching of the good news of God comes much closer to the presentation of an alternative world which counters the domination, the racism, the patriarchy which are such strong features still of the world in which we live.

## Preaching hopefully

The glimpses of a vision of preaching in this chapter show something of what I hope that preaching might be: based in the grassroots, real experiences where we find God, based in and building community, taking the risks that show God. These features, these glimpses, no complete picture in themselves, are the building blocks that enable me to preach with hope, both hope in God and hope in what preaching can do. I believe that preaching is important and makes a difference. It can be God's vehicle and can express God, and it does that best when the preacher is attentive to human beings who in their contexts strive to interpret the Bible and Christian tradition for today. Preaching is part of the ritual of remembering that helps us to interpret the present and inspires the future. I find preaching an assertive, definite, tentative and provisional activity, all at the same time. I find it one of the hardest of tasks, and one of the most rewarding.

And here, at the very end, I find myself searching for symbols which express preaching. Two unhelpful symbols come to mind first, which do encapsulate certain, perhaps caricatured, images of preaching. One symbol is the orator, the figure declaiming. I even have an image of this figure with head and arm upraised, and I admit the figure is male. It is a symbol which suggests that the action is all one way, *from* the preacher, *to* the congregation. One side is active, the other passively receives (and there's a stereotyped, gendered association!). This symbol, on the other hand, concentrates on the manner of delivery and the figure of the preacher, both of which I have needed to do on occasion in this book.

The second rather unhelpful symbol of preaching is the pulpit. The pulpit represents a significant space, a significant place, and an expectancy about what might happen through or from that space. But it can be representative also of containment, and a sign of separation between preacher and congregation. It is even something to cling on to for support, but often the wrong kind of support.

A better symbol of preaching, for me, is the invitation. It has deliberate overtones of the evangelistic appeal, but it also taps into the frequent, ordinary experiences of receiving invitations. 'Come and join in'; 'come on down!'; 'join us at our party'. The invitation creates anticipation and excitement at best, and a feeling of being special.    An invitation always comes as something profoundly personal: *your* company is wanted.   But it is an invitation to come and join with others, to be part of a celebrating community.   In defining the aim of preaching as enabling the recognition of God's work, Donald English also went on to the next stage which was that preaching allows people to see how to become involved in God's work (see note 1 above).   The advantage of the symbol of an invitation is that it is profoundly incomplete until the person invited responds in some way.   The invitation is to become involved with God and involved with God's work, and our preaching is directed to the response to God we cannot determine but for which we can hope.

Hope is the expression of vision and direction which believes in a good future based on God's promises and articulates how the anticipated future promises of God are already being experienced.   Again, that is the theology that affects the manner and content of our preaching.   To preach hopefully, we need to develop and hold on to our own vision for preaching, our own hopes for preaching. Then we will have something to move on with, in accordance with God's purposes, towards God's presence.

# EPILOGUE

Do women preach differently from men? Why should there be a distinctive women's perspective on preaching? Why should women preachers be treated somehow separately from men in this series? Shouldn't there be 'a man's perspective on preaching' in this series? I have been asked all these questions and more over the period of time I have spent writing this book. The comments and questions came even thicker and faster when the subject of this book became clear from the publicity for the series as a whole. Some of these questions have been asked with more seriousness of purpose than others!

In her American context, Christine Smith suggests many women are hopeful about preaching, because preaching gives significance for their naming of reality and their faith experience.[1] I am not sure that the preachers I have spoken with would give that sort of reasoning for their hope in preaching. When I asked a question about the possible distinctiveness of women's preaching in the questionnaires and conversations I have referred to before, many of those asked did want to label some things as more characteristic of women's preaching. A rootedness in experience, inclusivity, creativity were all mentioned. But almost all the respondents also felt that the notion of anything distinctive was problematic: men as well as women preachers could show these characteristics, and women as well as men could fail to show them. Generalisations were identified more clearly in what were felt to be congregational expectations of women as preachers. When answering questions about themselves as preachers, the respondents, even those particularly conscious of gender issues, or those who would happily label themselves 'feminist', characterised their own preaching and models of preaching in individual rather than gendered terms. That chimes in with what I have done.

To any bald question about the differences between men and women as preachers, the answer must be there aren't any. More nuanced questions and answers might elicit differences in perception about women preachers, or even different starting points between women and men because of some socialised experiences or expectations. But differences in socialisation as women and men would have to be looked at amidst the complex of many other influences on us as social beings, in which gender is not the only factor. It might be that other factors of sameness or dissimilarity have more influence on preaching – for instance, class and education, or aspects of cultural allegiance. There are physical differences between women and men, and that is about as far as I would want to go in talking about absolute differences between the two sexes (although some scholars would want to problematise those differences also). But when it comes to preaching, even physical differences such as timbre and pitch of voice do not line up absolutely either side of a thick dividing line between women and men. And none of these differences will necessarily line up with differences of outcome in preaching. There are undoubtedly some anecdotes, pointing to some tendencies which might separate many women preachers from many men, but there is nothing scientifically decisive about them. For every stereotype we will find a significant exception: significant enough, I hope, to make us challenge what we thought was a rule in the first place. So, I argue that, since women preachers are in themselves as varied as their male counterparts, their preaching will vary similarly.

I have not attempted in this book to describe a distinctive women's perspective on preaching or the practice of preaching which would cover all women, and mark women out as different from men. All I have attempted is to describe preaching from my own perspective, *recognising that my own perspective is gendered.*

That same perspective can be defined in many other ways, and it is individual. The way I explore any issue, and the way I have explored preaching, allows for this interplay between me as a unique individual and various 'categories' or contexts or communities, which form standards and expectations which I may take as my patterns, or which I may kick against. All of us, preachers or not, conscious of it or not, are doing the same.

# NOTES

## Chapter 1

1. Jane Craske, The Fernley-Hartley Lecture 1999, 'Seeing Visions, Hearing Voices: The Consequences of Feminist Perspectives in Theology', *Epworth Review*, 26:3, 1999, pp.12-24.

2. Rebecca Chopp, *Saving Work: Feminist Practices of Theological Education*, Louisville, Westminster John Knox Press, 1995, p.4.

3. Thomas H Troeger, *The Parable of Ten Preachers*, Nashville, Abingdon Press, 1992, p.13.

4. Patricia Wilson-Kastner, *Imagery for Preaching*, Minneapolis, Fortress Press, 1989, p.13.

5. Colin Morris, *Raising The Dead: The Art of the Preacher as Public Performer*, London, Fount (HarperCollins), 1996.

6. Susan J White, 'A New Story to Live By?', *Transmission*, Bible Society, Spring 1998, p.4.

7. Gerd Theissen, *The Sign Language of Faith: Opportunities for Preaching Today*, London, SCM Press, 1998, p.59.

## Chapter 2

1. W E Sangster, *The Craft of Sermon Construction*, London, Epworth Press, 1949, p.90.

2. W E Sangster, *The Craft of Sermon Illustration*, London, Epworth Press, 1946, pp.56-57.

3. Robert Adler, 'Pigeonholed', *New Scientist*, 167:2258, 30th September 2000, pp.38-41.

4. Joan Smith, *Different for Girls*, London, Vintage, 1998, pp.xii-xiii.

5. Mary Wollstonecraft, *A Vindication of the Rights of Woman*, first published 1792.

6. Anthropologist Margaret Mead, quoted in Dale Spender, *Men's Studies Modified*, Oxford and Elmsford, New York, Pergamon, 1981, p.1.

7. Anne Borrowdale, *Distorted Images: Christian Attitudes to Women, Men and Sex*, London, SPCK, 1991, p.1.


## Chapter 3

1. Elizabeth Cady Stanton, *The Woman's Bible*, first published 1895 & 1898, Boston, Northeastern University Press, 1993.

2. Ibid p.12.

3. Ibid p.21.

4. Ibid p.125.

5. See, for instance, Katie G Cannon, 'The Emergence of Black Feminist Consciousness' in Letty M Russell, *Feminist Interpretation of the Bible*, Blackwell, 1985, and Nancy L Eisland, *The Disabled God: Toward a Liberatory Theology of Disability*, Nashville, Abingdon Press, 1994, chapter 4.

6. Most well-known for this is Phyllis Trible, *Texts of Terror: Literary-Feminist Readings of Biblical Narratives*, Philadelphia, Fortress Press, 1984.

7. Luise Schottroff, *Lydia's Impatient Sisters: A Feminist Social History of Early Christianity*, London, SCM Press, 1995, p.xv.

8. Elisabeth Schüssler Fiorenza, *In Memory of Her*, London, SCM Press, 1983, p.50.

9. Susan J White, 'The Craft of Sermon Illustration Revisited', *Epworth Review*, 24:1, 1997, p.53.

10. Gerd Theissen, *The Sign Language of Faith*, p.30.

11. Ibid p.39.

12. In *Sisters in the Wilderness*, Delores Williams argues something similar about how African-American women might interact with the Bible. She takes the Hagar tradition as an important metaphor, that focuses on God enabling survival, rather than liberation. She links that into African-American women's slavery and post-slavery experiences in America. Methodologically, she lines up with *and critiques* black male liberation theology, and she lines up with *and critiques* white feminist theology. D Williams, *Sisters in the Wilderness: The Challenge of Womanist God-Talk*, Maryknoll, New York Orbis Books, 1993.

## Chapter 4

1. Kathleen Fischer, *Women at the Well: Feminist Perspectives on Spiritual Direction*, London, SPCK, 1989.

2. Mark Pryce, *Finding a Voice: Men, Women and the Community of the Church*, London, SCM Press, 1996, p.99.

3. Leonard Swidler, 'Jesus was a Feminist', *The Catholic World*, January 1971, pp.177-183.

4. Glenna Jackson, 'Jesus as First-Century Feminist: Christian Anti-Judaism?', *Feminist Theology*, 19, 1998, pp.85-98.

5.  Dorothy L Sayers, 'The Human-Not-Quite-Human', in *Unpopular Opinions*, Gollancz, 1946; now used as the epigraph in H Ward, J Wild, J Morley eds., *Celebrating Women*, London, SPCK, 1995, p.1.

6.  Mary Daly, *Beyond God the Father: Toward a Philosophy of Women's Liberation*, first published 1973, London, The Women's Press, 1986, p.73.

7.  D W Cleverley Ford, *Preaching Today*, Epworth Press and SPCK, 1969, pp.23-25.

8.  Rosemary Radford Ruether, *Sexism and God-Talk*, SCM Press, 1983.

9.  Teresa Berger, 'A Female Christ Child in the Manger and a Woman on the Cross, Or: The Historicity of the Jesus Event and the Inculturation of the Gospel', *Feminist Theolgy*, 11, 1996, pp.32-45.

**Chapter 5**

1.  Marjorie Dobson, 'Women and Worship', *Worship Live*, 13, Spring 1999, p.11.

2.  George Eliot, *Adam Bede*, first published 1859, London, J M Dent and Sons Ltd., 1906, pp.23-24.

3.  Ibid p.515.

4.  Bettye Collier-Thomas, *Daughters of Thunder: Black Women Preachers and their Sermons*, San Francisco, Jossey-Bass, 1998.

5.  Margaret Batty, 'Origins: The Age of Wesley', in *Workaday Preachers: The Story of Methodist Local Preaching*, eds., Geoffrey Milburn and Margaret Batty, Methodist Publishing House, 1995, p.11.

6.  E Dorothy Graham, 'Women Local Preachers', in *Workaday Preachers*, p.184.

7.   Christine M Smith, *Weaving The Sermon: Preaching in Feminist Perspective*, Louisville, Westminster John Knox Press, 1989, p.63.

**Chapter 6**

1.   Donald English, *An Evangelical Theology of Preaching*, Nashville, Abingdon Press, 1996, chapter 1.

2.   Patricia Wilson-Kastner, *Imagery for Preaching*, p.12.

**Epilogue**

1.   Christine Smith, *Weaving The Sermon*, p.108.